A SKEPTIC'S GUIDE TO GOD

Lori —
To a new friend and beautiful person. I'm not trying to convert you with this book — it is simply the most biographical about myself — which I would like to share with you.
God bless you

Also by Larkin Spivey

God in the Trenches

Miracles of the American Revolution

Battlefields and Blessings: Stories of Faith and Courage from World War II

Stories of Faith and Courage from the Korean War

Stories of Faith and Courage from the Vietnam War

A SKEPTIC'S GUIDE TO GOD

BY

LARKIN SPIVEY

A Skeptic's Guide to God
Copyright © 2014 by Larkin Spivey
Published by CreateSpace

All rights reserved. Except for brief quotations in printed reviews, no part of this publication may be reproduced, stored in a retrieval system, or transmitted in any form or by any means (printed, written, photocopied, visual electronic, audio, or otherwise) without the prior permission of the author.

ISBN: 1494848473
ISBN 13: 9781494848477
Library of Congress Control Number: 2014900066
CreateSpace Independent Publishing Platform
North Charleston, South Carolina

Unless otherwise indicated, Bible quotations are taken from *The Holy Bible, New International Version (NIV)*. Copyright © 1973, 1978, and 1984 by International Bible Society. Used by permission of Zondervan Publishing House. All rights reserved.

Cover cartoon by Frank Cotham. This and other *New Yorker Collection* cartoons reprinted with permission of Conde Nast/The Cartoon Bank.

DEDICATION

To Joe Jarrett, Ben Martin, Jimmy Merritt, Garnett Ramsbottom, Frank Sloan, and Macky Singleton.

I have been blessed to be included in a small group with these close friends for more than fifteen years, meeting faithfully to study scripture, pray, talk about our concerns, and listen to each other. We have each been supported by the others through the joys and trials of marriage, fatherhood, and life in a challenging world.

These men have many gifts. Thoughtful, strong willed, fun loving, intellectual, erudite, outgoing, and complex are some of the traits that come to mind. Each possesses his own unique blend of skepticism and faithfulness that has been a constant source of inspiration to me in writing this book. I pray that God will grant to each of these men and each of their family members "a humble heart, a steadfast purpose, and a joyful hope."[1]

TABLE OF CONTENTS

FOREWORD xi
INTRODUCTION: SPIRITUAL BUT NOT RELIGIOUS xv

PART ONE: A Skeptic's Journey
- Chapter One — An Old Testament Household — 1
- Chapter Two — Leaving God Behind — 5
- Chapter Three — The Marine Corps as a Spiritual Mission — 12
- Chapter Four — A Decision to Love — 18
- Chapter Five — An Apostle of Maslow — 22
- Chapter Six — Going through the Episcopal Motions — 27
- Chapter Seven — Hard Times for a Skeptic — 32

PART TWO: A Side Journey into Science
- Chapter Eight — The Watchmaker God — 37
- Chapter Nine — Why Are So Many Physicists Believers? — 39
- Chapter Ten — Why Are So Many Biologists Atheists? — 45
- Chapter Eleven — What about the Information? — 51
- Chapter Twelve — The *Evolution* of Human Beings — 58
- Chapter Thirteen — "You Are Nothing but a Pack of Neurons" — 64
- Chapter Fourteen — A Summary of the Science — 72
- Chapter Fifteen — Is There Proof God Exists? — 79

PART THREE: What about the Bible?
- Chapter Sixteen — How Good Is the Good Book? — 85
- Chapter Seventeen — A New Look at the Old Testament — 88
- Chapter Eighteen — And Then Came the New Testament — 97

PART FOUR: A Skeptic's Favorite Objections
    Chapter Nineteen   The Dark Side   111
    Chapter Twenty   Hard Questions   119

PART FIVE: A New Journey
    Chapter Twenty-One   A Skeptic's Worst Moment   131
    Chapter Twenty-Two   The Anatomy of a Step of Faith   136
    Chapter Twenty-Three   Decisions, Decisions   138
    Chapter Twenty-Four   Beyond Nice   145

BIBLIOGRAPHY   151
NOTES   157
ABOUT THE AUTHOR   169

FOREWORD

People who possess a high degree of character and competence often see no need for God. Meeting the expectations of the world around them creates a sense of righteousness and self-sufficiency. So, when they are asked to recognize a higher authority in human affairs, the response is often ambivalence. They have various intellectual issues, are skeptical, and not inclined to quick judgments. Above all they consider themselves moral people.

Larkin Spivey has followed such a path, and this book is a clear and thoughtful recording of his journey as he struggled with all the objections that reason brings to the question of belief. His character and competence were indeed the greatest obstacles to his eventual commitment. Larkin comes from a prominent family in South Carolina with a distinguished history that placed on him a mantle of duty and honorable conduct at an early age. His life was filled with sparkling and unblemished achievements. He graduated from The Citadel with every possible honor. As Regimental Commander, he led the South Carolina Corps of Cadets. His academic record was stellar—a fact that contributes, no doubt, to the lucid read that follows. As a Marine officer, he served in the Cuban missile crisis, in the Dominican Republic intervention, and in Vietnam, where he fought at Khe Sanh, garnering awards for bravery and meritorious service in every venue. Later he was assigned to the prestigious Marine Barracks in Washington, DC, and served as a White House aide. After twenty years of distinguished service to the Marine Corps and the nation, Lieutenant Colonel Spivey retired from active duty and returned to his native South Carolina low country to begin a new career.

His pattern of success continued in a variety of business ventures. He developed and operated a recreational vehicle resort in Myrtle Beach, South Carolina, that ranks among the top in the nation. He also operates a real-estate development company and was a founder and director of a national bank. Because of his leadership ability, he has served on a variety of local and state association boards. In his church he was elected to the vestry, and he has served as lay rector and Secretariat member of Cursillos in Christianity and on the President's Council of the Luis Palau Evangelistic Association.

Larkin Spivey's personal life reflects similar success. He has been happily married for more than forty years to Lani Hillwig of Allentown, Pennsylvania. They both take pride in the successful lives of their four children and ten grandchildren.

Throughout these milestones of achievement, Larkin was also investigating and resolving the intellectual issues he addresses so well in the following chapters. As the reader will see, it was a terrific struggle, as each of his achievements reinforced the notion that he could formulate and execute his own life's purpose. But God was faithful throughout and finally led him to the point where he could glory in nothing "save the cross of our Lord Jesus Christ." How grateful we are that he yielded to the Holy Spirit's call. We now have this wonderful story and very useful guide to help other skeptics in their search for peace with God and to serve as a resource for believers trying to encourage skeptics they know.

> Major General John S. Grinalds
> United States Marine Corps (retired)
> Eighteenth President of The Citadel

A NOTE FOR SKEPTICS

In an effort to appeal to skeptics' often offbeat sense of humor, I have included quotes and definitions at the beginning of each chapter reflecting the often dark and devious perspectives of some of our most-renowned skeptics. Prominent among these are Ambrose Bierce and his famous *Devil's Dictionary* and Rick Bayan's *The Cynic's Dictionary*. Details of these and other unusual references are included in the footnotes and bibliography. I have also included throughout the book selected cartoons from *The New Yorker* reflecting the unique insights of some of our greatest cartoonists.

> **Religion**, n. Man's attempt to explain God, much to God's annoyance.[2]

> "Large skepticism leads to large understanding. Small skepticism leads to small understanding. No skepticism leads to no understanding."
> —Xi Zhi[3]

INTRODUCTION

Spiritual but Not Religious[4]

Although this book is titled *A Skeptic's Guide*, I have to admit I don't have a precise definition for the word *skeptic*. One of my favorites is "an idealist whose rose-colored glasses have been removed, snapped in two, and stomped into the ground, immediately improving his vision."[5] Dictionaries give a less fanciful picture of someone who is doubtful and questioning of the assertions of others, particularly in the area of religion. This covers a broad spectrum.

There is an ever-growing number of people seeking spiritual truth in areas outside what we know as traditional or organized religion.[6] More and more young people have no experience in the home or early life with matters of faith. There are also those going through what my daughter calls the "quarter-life crisis," during which a newly independent twenty-five-year-old experiences disillusionment with his or her childhood religion. Many others have disappointing experiences with religious organizations or the people in them at other times in life. Sometimes there is a break with religion due to a midlife crisis or some other painful event. There are also those outside organized religion who simply believe that the search for spiritual truth is an individual process of intellectual inquiry and don't want input from *any* higher authority.

You may fit one of these categories, or you may not. You probably resist being categorized at all. However, if you have doubts and unanswered questions about the ultimate purpose of your life, I hope you will keep reading. You may not have these doubts, but you may be trying to encourage or understand someone else who does. I hope you too will find something useful in these pages.

Even though the term may be difficult to define, the skeptic I identify with does not relate to the concept of faith or belief in anything merely because it is traditional or widely accepted. This person has an active intellectual life and seeks answers to the big questions in his or her own way. Modern science, philosophy, and a devotion to human reason have played roles in leading this person away from any formal or even informal religious system that requires blind acceptance of any set of beliefs. In fact, more and more are taught that the idea of belief itself is passé, as a recent scientific paper on DNA stated: "We tell our first-year undergraduates, 'Belief is the curse of the thinking class.'"[7]

If you consider yourself a member in good standing with the "thinking class," I hope my story will help you find a different perspective. The message of this book is based on the opposite assumption. If your life is going to have meaning and purpose, you *have* to believe in something. If you believe in something important, your purpose will be important. If you are interested in an ultimate purpose, you have to seek something ultimately important. I believe that the object of such a search has to be God. If there is an intelligent designer of the universe, there is at least the possibility of an ultimate meaning for it. In seeking to understand your purpose, you have to come to some understanding of God.

This book is in part an autobiographical sketch of my journey in search of answers to this question. I present this not because I think my life has been so interesting or that I enjoy relating it. In fact, I'm very uncomfortable using myself as a subject. I know that many of my *profound*

INTRODUCTION

insights are blinding glimpses of the obvious to others. Despite these reservations I believe that a personal account serves a purpose. A story is often the best way to convey certain ideas. Other subjects need more straightforward information and even argument. Both of these means are intertwined through this book, with Parts Two through Five a little heavier on the factual content—which skeptics will probably prefer.

So, in this book, you will find a story and a certain amount of information. If you are my kind of skeptic, your life is already an information-gathering process. In fact, you may be suffering from *too much* information. The critical question is: how do we get from information *about* something to belief *in* something? I have been motivated to write this book to explain how this can happen. It was not an easy process for me, and I don't think it is easy for any skeptical person. For some it takes a profound crisis or devastating experience in their lives. Some have to reach a low point with nowhere else to turn. I offer my own story to show that it can happen also as the end result of an open-minded search for truth.

I need to let you know upfront that I became a Christian at age fifty-three, after a long life of skepticism. I have been a career Marine Corps officer, businessman, writer, husband, and father. I am not a theologian or member of the clergy. Whenever I write or speak, others who are skeptical about religion are always at the forefront of my thoughts. I assure you that in this book, I will not assume you share any of my beliefs.

PART ONE

A Skeptic's Journey

> **Childhood**, n. The period of human life intermediate between the idiocy of infancy and the folly of youth—two removes from the sin of manhood and three from the remorse of age.[8]

CHAPTER ONE

An Old Testament Household

I've always been a skeptic. When I once came across the definition "a person disposed to an attitude of doubt," I knew I had found a label for myself. I was a twelve-year-old Boy Scout who never fell for the so-called Snipe Hunt. On my first camping trip, volunteers were recruited to hold a bag at the end of a long ditch so everyone else could drive a mysterious little critter called a snipe down this ditch into the waiting bag. This could be done only between one and four in the morning because that was when the furry little creature came out. No thanks. Subconsciously I already knew what it meant to be left "holding the bag."

On another dark night, there was the Branding Ceremony. I found myself standing in line blindfolded, waiting my turn for the final act of induction into the Order of the Arrow. I heard screams down the line as others were seared by the dreaded red hot arrow tip. I wasn't fooled, even though a brief flash of panic hit me involuntarily as someone splashed melted candle wax on my bare forearm. At least the skeptic didn't pass out.

My religious upbringing had a similar flavor. I often had the sense I was being manipulated into falling for something. I was always eager to learn and full of questions about God and the Bible, but the answers to my "why" questions were often: "It says so in the Bible" or "You just have to have faith." These were the wrong answers for a young skeptic. I kept asking myself, "If you don't have faith, where do you get it?" Somehow I managed to go for more than five decades without finding an answer.

My inner revolts didn't disturb my outward demeanor as an obedient and even reverent young person. As a typical product of my time and place, I seldom questioned my parents or teachers on any issues of daily life or behavior. Conway, South Carolina, during the 1940s and 1950s was an idyllic setting for a young person. Walking home from grade school, there were always new adventures waiting in a small town with woods, swamps, and the Waccamaw River to explore. I took charge of my own boat for my first solo expedition at the age of ten.

Saturday mornings were reserved for Western movies at the Carolina Theater on Main Street. The plots, heroes, and villains were always consistent. The Lone Ranger was the toughest man in the West and at the same time the epitome of kindness. His lonely and mysterious quest to do good was usually misunderstood and little appreciated. In these dramas the good guys struggled and won, the villains were defeated, and crime never paid.

Looking back, the movies and most other institutions of society all played roles in shaping young people for the better. Popular music was benign, movies and radio programs adhered to certain moral standards, and television came along too late to do any real harm. Also, outside play was the most important activity in town for the grade-school set. From high school on, there was work to do. It may be hard to believe now, but children then were *not* the focus of their parents' lives. I have often felt that my own parents had it way too easy.

I was raised in the Presbyterian Church even though my mother and father were Methodists. I owed this to my grandmother Norton, who was the daughter of a Presbyterian minister. Even though she allowed her daughter to marry and become a Methodist, she took care of the

AN OLD TESTAMENT HOUSEHOLD

grandchildren's religious upbringing herself. This did not seem especially noteworthy at the time. We all just "went to church." There were certainly no doctrinal disputes between these mainline denominations. Only the Baptists were viewed as different due to their tendency to be somewhat overzealous in their spirituality.

The Spivey household was organized on the Old Testament model. There was the law, and there was judgment. I don't remember questioning either. My father, Bayliss, was an industrious man like his father, Colonel D. Allen Spivey. They were both businessmen, bankers, and political figures. My dad was also the town's fire chief. He often quoted Robert E. Lee: "Duty is the sublimest word in the English language." My dad had his duties, and his children had theirs. This was not so much a matter of discipline or blind obedience to authority as it was just doing the right thing.

"Bad timing—he's in one of his Old Testament moods today."

Charles Barsotti[9]

Purpose in life was not a matter of introspection. Purpose was found in life's obligations, and every obligation was a serious matter. My mother, G (for Genewood), completed the family formula for life with her definition of happiness: "a byproduct of duty well performed." If you are ever frustrated by or depressed about the unsuccessful "pursuit of happiness," you might try this out. My mother would grant you the right to happiness after you took care of your obligations. This formula is probably better for most than antidepressants or psychiatrists.

My image of God fit this family pattern. The Supreme Being was a remote and benevolent figure with high expectations. He wasn't that concerned with my personal struggle in life and didn't intend to engage in a lot of communication on the subject. I occasionally talked to him but was never conscious of being heard. Even so, I knew he was aware of what I was doing and always expected me to do the right thing. I could only worry and wonder if I was.

During those early years, my tools for facing life began to take shape. I had a strong work ethic energized by a highly developed Presbyterian conscience and frequent doubts if I were working hard enough. I felt I had a lot to prove. These traits made for a good student and overachiever in many activities and an introspective person seeking answers to a lot of questions.

> Education is the path from cocky ignorance to miserable uncertainty.
>
> —Mark Twain[10]

CHAPTER TWO

Leaving God Behind

The first challenge to my fragile worldview came in college. Professors seemed to take pleasure in undermining anything resembling religious belief. In that era, I believe many were seeking to broaden the horizons of their students. However, there was a bias in many academic disciplines against religion. There was an underlying assumption that science had explained the natural processes that govern the physical world and had rendered biblical accounts of creation and the concept of an intervening god irrelevant to modern life.

In accordance with family tradition, I reported to military college at The Citadel. I was seventeen. I had an unfair advantage over most of my contemporaries in that I never considered going anywhere else, never questioned the so-called "system," and was generally scared to death. The first time I walked into my new environment, however, I noticed a well-buffed brass plaque in the front sally port of Number Four barracks: "Duty is the sublimest word in the English language. Robert E. Lee." I almost felt at home. Paradoxically, the young men who choose The Citadel usually are the ones who need it least, who already have some sense of duty and self-discipline. In retrospect, I put my sons and me in that category.

My favorite teacher was an enthusiastic young English professor named H. B. Alexander. He talked about the great ideas in literature and was the best at challenging grand assertions, whether from great writers or lowly students. He could recite passages and poems with great passion and was full of provocative insights. I developed a deep interest in poetry and what was often referred to as "mystical experience" and can still recite William Butler Yeats's "Sailing to Byzantium." My freshman interpretation of this classic was that religion had become a "tattered coat upon a stick," and the eternal was to be found only in Yeats's "monuments of unaging intellect."[11] Such poetry seemed to be a complex code challenging me to decipher its multiple and mysterious meanings. Given my brand of skepticism, I always preferred wrestling with difficult concepts rather than plain truths. This set the pattern of my inquiry for years to come.

Another favorite work was *The Rubáiyát of Omar Khayyám*, which was full of insights along these lines:

> *I sent my Soul through the Invisible,*
> *Some letter of that After-life to spell:*
> *And by and by my Soul return'd to me,*
> *And answer'd "I Myself am Heav'n and Hell."*[12]

This made a lot more sense to me than most biblical passages. I was amazed one day to hear my father assert that "the moving finger writes, and having writ, moves on…" I don't think I ever heard him quote from another poem. His opinion about poets was that they seemed to have difficulty expressing clear thoughts. He made an exception for *The Rubáiyát* and indirectly confirmed a certain seldom-expressed skepticism of his own.

As my mental life was unfolding, my physical life at The Citadel revolved around repeated boot-camp experiences. The plebe system lasted the complete freshman year. The military routines of drill, formations, parades, inspections, and physical fitness training were carried out under constant mental pressure to be stronger, faster, and more efficient. This forceful supervision, with a measure of pure harassment thrown in, was meant to form our character, build unity with classmates, and teach us how to function under extreme pressure. As if one year of this weren't enough, I later volunteered for the Junior Sword Drill and Summerall Guards, elite drill teams with their own time-honored rites of passage and training methods. Again, mental and physical stress was the order of the day throughout the process of selecting and training those of us who would have to perform these intricate ceremonies perfectly in every situation. In every military and academic endeavor, my drive to prove myself remained strong. This, and a large measure of good fortune, eventually led to my appointment as Regimental Commander, the ultimate military achievement I could then envision as a Citadel cadet.

During that time my spiritual life continued on its superficial plain. Religious services were still mandatory at The Citadel, so I spent most Sunday mornings in Summerall Chapel, usually going through the motions. I continued to consider myself a basically good person and felt I was doing my duty toward God by living up to life's obligations, including occasional appearances in church.

A few days before my twenty-first birthday, I accepted my diploma from General Mark Clark and was sworn in as a Marine Corps officer. This was one of those milestone days in life that I didn't fully appreciate at the time. Like finishing high school, it was an accomplishment, but again I was headed from the top of one organization to the bottom of the next. I knew the Marine Corps would be a challenge, and I could sense a purposeful direction in my life. It would take some time for this purpose to clarify and become deeply meaningful.

As I expected, my tests and trials were renewed when I joined the Marine Corps. First there was the Platoon Leaders Class (aka Officer Candidate School) at Quantico, Virginia, where I found out the "candidates" weren't there to be trained so much as weeded out. We ran the infamous Hill Trail several times a day and were subjected to forced marches in full combat gear all over the vast base. These so-called hikes were meant to be walked at an extremely fast pace but instead demanded almost constant running to close up the column. The heat, dust, thirst, and pain were unremitting. The staff showed no mercy to stragglers, and every day our ranks grew thinner. These measures were a pure test of determination and resulted in a much-reduced graduating class with some understanding of the commitment it would take to be Marines.

One day our drill instructor, Sergeant "Ski," told us about losing his rifle-cleaning kit during combat operations in Korea. He had only a toothbrush on hand, so he used that for weeks to keep his rifle functioning. The concept of putting a clean rifle ahead of oral hygiene was not an easy one for a group of college boys to comprehend. However, this story came back to me often in combat as I reexamined my own personal priorities. I often left behind many comfort items, food included, to make room for extra ammunition and water.

As a young Marine lieutenant, I continued to attend church services, often in the field when there was a chaplain present. One day a fellow officer asked me why I bothered, since I didn't seem to believe too much of what was being said. I recall responding that I was at least around other people interested in something above and beyond themselves. This might still be a pretty good reason for anyone to go to church occasionally.

My prayer life, such as it was, came to something of a climax on a clear spring day in the North Carolina mountains. I had a lot on my mind as I drove across the state from Camp Lejeune to Brevard. I had to make one of my first decisions in life about the long-range future. I had joined the Marine Corps as a reserve officer with a three-year commitment, expecting to get on with some other career after that. However, I had recently received the opportunity to augment into the Regular Marine Corps and accept a career position.

After sweating my way up Looking Glass Mountain, I found a large rock bathed in sunshine with an expanse of deep blue sky and an unlimited view. For the hundredth time, I weighed the pros and cons of my options: law school, business school, business opportunities, the Corps. I appealed to God at some point for his input. I prayed passionately. My life was at a crossroads; I perceived certain options, but in fact any option would be open if he were to make it known. I tried sincerely to put my life in his hands. I didn't know how I might hear his answer to this plea since I had never consciously heard an answer before. I heard nothing this time either and finally gave up in frustration.

Dana Fradon[14]

Instead of a voice from above, a poem came to mind that I had memorized in my Citadel English class: "Invictus." In this time-honored work, William E. Henley penned the immortal phrase:

> *It matters not how strait the gate,*
> *How charged with punishments the scroll,*
> *I am the master of my fate:*
> *I am the captain of my soul.*[13]

That day on the mountaintop, I concluded God had no interest in my decisions, and devoting time and energy to studying and trying to understand him was not a useful purpose. If he existed at all, he would continue a distant authority figure and future judge. In light of the many successes up to that point in my life, being the "captain of my soul" seemed the ideal stance for the journey ahead.

Around that time I came across Ayn Rand when I randomly picked *The Fountainhead* off a bookstore shelf. She was what I would call an angry atheist, portraying most human misery as the result of oppressive governments and organized religion emphasizing the selfish, sinful nature of man. Her villains were politicians, clergymen, bureaucrats, social workers, and anyone who laid claim to the fruits of others' efforts. Her heroes were architects, inventors, and industrialists who produced the wealth of the world.

I found her themes compelling, especially her criticisms of big government and organized religion. Although I remained unconvinced about atheism, her books strongly reinforced my agnosticism. She had the answer to one of my long-standing questions about the nature of selfishness, portrayed in my early Sunday schools as a sinful quality to be suppressed. I had figured out that trying to do good to get into heaven involved basically selfish motives. Rand resolved this question by proclaiming that man's first duty was to himself, portraying all human progress as the result of man's selfish pursuit of his own interests within the bounds of law and ethics.

There are some blind spots in Rand's worldview, but at the time her influence strengthened my professionalism and commitment to the Marine Corps. This commitment gave my life full meaning and purpose, as I was saw it at that time. There was striving for excellence and the ever-present mission of preparing myself to fight in defense of my nation. The Marine Corps was a total physical and intellectual commitment. It provided a higher, even spiritual calling to my life. I remained interested in religion and philosophy from an intellectual point of view, but the focus of my life would be infantry tactics and strategy.

These experiences early in my career confirmed more than ever my skepticism toward religion and religious assertions about God. I was convinced such skepticism was an appropriate stance for a man of the modern world. As the "master of my fate," I would find my meaning and purpose in such things as duty, honor, country, and Corps. For more than thirty years, the possibility that God may have answered my mountaintop prayer or worked in some way to influence my professional decisions never once crossed my mind.

> You can't say that civilizations don't advance... in every war they kill you in a new way.
> —Will Rogers[15]

> Experience is a hard teacher because she gives the test first, the lessons afterward.
> —Vernon Sanders Law[16]

CHAPTER THREE

The Marine Corps as a Spiritual Mission

Occasionally, when friends find out I am a retired Marine, they say, "You just don't seem like the Marine type." They say their image of a Marine is more assertive and aggressive than I seem to be. They're probably right. One of my senior officers went to bat for me early in my career to help me get into the highly selective Second Force Reconnaissance Company. The commander of that company, the well-known Pat Carouthers, asserted: "I want an officer who will 'walk through that wall' if I tell him to!" My advocate replied, "Spivey would do that, but he would probably use the door." I always considered that a high compliment.

I never found thinking first a detriment to being an effective Marine, especially in Force Recon. For instance, there were often competing demands for initiative and obedience. There were moments when I had to follow disagreeable and sometimes dangerous orders. However, there were also many occasions when orders were not forthcoming, especially in the heat of combat. "Doing the right thing," even without direct orders, was often necessary. I frequently had to function independently and use creativity in solving problems.

In October 1962 I was executive officer, or second in command, of the Marine Detachment on the aircraft carrier USS *Randolph*. The ship was at sea for routine training operations off the Virginia coast when word came of a crisis in Cuba over the discovery of Soviet nuclear missiles. At the time my commanding officer was ashore with half the detachment for weapons training at Dam Neck, Virginia. The *Randolph* steamed south, and I didn't see my boss or the rest of the unit again for a month. I assumed duties as CO of the Marine Detachment and commander of the ship's landing/boarding party. My assigned task was to prepare a force of Marines and Sailors to occupy and search Soviet vessels at sea—a likely mission for our ship as part of the blockade force around Cuba. As a twenty-two-year-old second lieutenant a few months out of Basic School, I had to face the prospect of boarding a Soviet ship and dealing with the consequences. I was extremely conscious of the fact that my newly organized unit might be responsible for starting World War III.

Reconnaissance officers also had to function independently. We were trained in deep patrolling far behind enemy lines, requiring mastery of parachute and submarine entry and extraction techniques. In 1965 I deployed to the Caribbean with my platoon in support of a battalion landing team embarked aboard amphibious ships. When communist rebels threatened the Dominican Republic, we went on full alert. We drew ammunition and prepared parachutes for a night jump into a drop zone near Santo Domingo.

To my great disappointment, the night combat jump did not prove necessary. Instead we went in with the first wave of helicopters to secure and operate a landing zone near the American embassy. As usual I was given broad latitude in carrying out my assigned mission. It still amazes me to recall many of the things I did as a Marine lieutenant.

Marine officers also had to find the balance between the mission and the men. There were tough missions that often required tough measures to accomplish, and I always pushed hard to get the job done. They say leadership in combat is simple. The corollary to this is the fact that in combat, the simple things are always hard to do. It often took harsh measures to keep young Marines from needlessly endangering themselves and to force attention to the mundane details of noise discipline, camouflage, and personal hygiene. I was always amazed by how invincible most of my men thought they were. That self-confidence, however, is part of what has always made Marines so special. Leading them was a challenge but also a privilege of the highest order.

Although the mission was paramount, nothing could be accomplished without motivated troops. The Marine Corps approach to this truth entails the ethic of the servant leader. In every situation, where humanly possible, the needs of the men are considered first. Every Marine knows that his officers will do everything they can to minimize the risks and look after the needs of those under them. Marine units have always been successful because this trust prevails during the tough and dangerous times.

Prophetically, my father once gave me some advice on leadership: "It says in the Bible, 'If you would be first among them, you must be servant to all.'" I learned about forty years later that Jesus Christ made this statement; he went on to say, "For even the Son of Man did not come to be served, but to serve."[17] Amazingly I found this approach to leadership deeply ingrained, almost to the level of religious belief, within Marine Corps tradition.

Marines are rightly noted for toughness, an important trait on the battlefield. Although physical fitness is important, a sign often seen on barracks walls gives the true Marine perspective: "Toughness is a quality of mind without which physical conditioning is a mockery." In Vietnam one of my fellow company commanders had a sign over his bunker that expressed the same sentiment in a typically irreverent manner: "Yea, though I walk through the valley of the shadow of death, I will fear no evil—because I'm the toughest son of a bitch in the valley."

"It would be a shame if they surrendered before we had a chance to shoot this."

Jason Patterson[18]

I have to admit, a degree of youthful arrogance had set in at this stage of my life as I took great pride in what I perceived to be my physical and mental toughness. I had endured the various and seemingly unending trials of military college, Marine Corps training, Ranger and Airborne Schools, and Special Forces training and usually came out on top. At every turn those of us who made it through had to succeed in all missions in spite of adversity, from extreme fatigue and sleep deprivation to impossible terrain and severe weather. These trials were meant to teach certain military skills but were also designed to develop an ability to think and act calmly under pressure and in the midst of crisis. This process of enduring and overcoming challenges gave me a certain mental toughness and self-confidence that were important throughout my life, especially in military service. Unfortunately, unbounded self-confidence also tends to border on overconfidence and even arrogance, and this mind-set assuredly puts anyone at risk of inevitable disappointment. At the time, however, my motto from "Invictus" continued to serve me well as I looked to my skills to see me through the trials of combat.

A climax of sorts came to my character development on the slopes of Hill 861. Unfortunately I never stood on the summit of that mountain in the northwest corner of Vietnam, even though many unfortunate young Marines and I tried mightily. After other units had made scattered contact with North Vietnamese Army (NVA) units around the Khe Sanh combat base in early April 1967, my unit, Kilo Company, Third Battalion, Third Marines, was ordered to take the hill overlooking the base.

We moved gradually up the steep slope until we ran into an unsuspected complex of well-entrenched NVA units near the crest. Kilo Company took a lot of casualties in heavy fighting and was still below the summit at the end of the day. We spent a long night under constant mortar attack, digging in and nursing our wounded. The next morning, after another vicious firefight, my battalion commander, Lt. Col. Gary Wilder, came on the radio and asked the fateful question, "Can you take the hill?"

I had the conscious thought that this was one of those pivotal moments when heroes are made. However, I heard myself say, "Negative. We don't have the horsepower." Col. Wilder agreed, and we began the complicated process of getting off the hill. Part of my undying respect for helicopter pilots stems from the action that morning of two Huey gunships firing just over our heads as we alternated moving units down the hill with our casualties and our gear. Over the next few days, concentrated air strikes reduced Hill 861's elevation considerably. Other units later occupied the hill and continued the battle beyond.

I have replayed these events many times in my mind and have asked many questions of myself. Should I have recognized the strength of

THE MARINE CORPS AS A SPIRITUAL MISSION

the NVA position sooner and pulled back? Should I have pushed ahead harder? Why did I survive unscathed when so many of my men did not? These questions have no answers, but I cannot avoid the fact that I was responsible. Young Marines died, and we did not take the hill.

Up until that moment, my career had been marked by one success after another. I was not credited with failure for this battle on Hill 861. Some considered it a failure of intelligence in that more was not known about enemy dispositions that close to the combat base or that the North Vietnamese were in the advanced stages of a Dien Bien Phu like siege of Khe Sanh.[19] Even though there was no fault per se, for me this was not a success. It was pretty clear to me that I had not controlled these events and there was something governing my fate and that of many others besides myself.

This lesson seemed to present itself often on Vietnam battlefields. Men beside me fell while I was unscathed. Airstrikes veered momentarily offline and inflicted casualties on unsuspecting friendly troops. One man in the middle of a column leaned on a tree and was severely wounded by a mine that others had passed. It's hard to describe the feeling of being in a helicopter and seeing bullet holes appear around you from ground fire. These moments of vulnerability in the air lasted for minutes or seconds but always seemed like hours. This was random death or injury at its most stark.

They say there are no atheists in foxholes. This is probably true, although it doesn't say too much about the nature of this kind of faith. During my times in combat, I confess, I had some moments of intense prayer. However, I wasn't conscious of God answering my prayers then or of giving him credit for the outcome later. There was not even a glimmer of thought that he might have somehow played a role in my actions or decisions—or that he might even have been involved in bringing me safely through these events.

> By all means, marry. If you get a good wife, you'll become happy; if you get a bad one, you'll become a philosopher.
>
> —Socrates[20]

CHAPTER FOUR

A Decision to Love

I followed my tour of duty in Vietnam with a radical change in climate and a year's exposure to the cold, clear air of Canada. Professionally I was still on the fast track, with an assignment to Command and Staff College in Kingston, Ontario, followed by duty at the prestigious Marine Barracks in Washington, DC. There my troops performed ceremonial duties in the Washington area and provided security to the President, Camp David, and the Capitol building. After a rigorous screening process, I was also appointed as a White House social aide, charged with coordinating receptions, state dinners, bill signings, and other events involving visitors to the White House.

At that point in my career, marriage was not on my radar. I had seen enough bad unions and infidelity in foreign ports to confirm the benefits of bachelorhood. In fact there is an old saying in the Corps: "If the Marine Corps wanted you to have a wife, they would issue you one."

That picture changed when Lani Hillwig entered my life. At the time we both lived in a large apartment complex in Arlington, Virginia, and saw each other occasionally in passing. I was pretty shy about approaching such an attractive woman, and she had a reserved demeanor, not needing another man in her life at that time. One day, however, a mutual friend formally introduced us, and I worked up the courage to ask her out on a date. Love at first sight is not exactly a good description of what ensued.

Lani soon found out that if there was going to be conversation between us, she would have to do most of it, and she went through many frustrating periods waiting for me to open up with my inner thoughts. She had to wait even longer to get a hint of my feelings about her or anything else important to me. Meanwhile uncontainable passion and joy for life emanated from her. Fortunately she persisted in her effort to understand this overly reticent, career-focused Marine, and our relationship continued and slowly grew stronger.

My mother once told me that when considering a mate, you don't ask, can I live *with* this person? You have to know you can't live *without* her. I called Lani from the White House at 12:30 a.m. on August 5, 1970, about one minute after realizing this was exactly how I had come to feel about her. At that moment I made the most important decision of my life up to that time and asked her to marry me. By asking her over the telephone, I earned everlasting infamy in Spivey family lore for the most unromantic proposal ever made. This Yankee woman from Pennsylvania proved in every respect to be the sails for my boat and eventually for our larger family ship. I tried to be the rudder and even at times the anchor, but we wouldn't have gotten very far without our sails. Her passion and enthusiasm have always animated our family life.

Lani and I were married at the Fort Myer chapel in Arlington, Virginia. Since I was an officer at the Washington Marine Barracks, famous for its military ceremonies, we had the most precise military wedding ever seen at that army post. Amazingly the post chaplain allowed us to write our own wedding vows, for which we drew extensively on Kahlil Gibran. When we got to the part about "the pillars standing apart," Lani's mother squirmed a little in her seat. We also rejected the proviso about "until death do us part." We didn't give a lot of theological thought to the question, but we instinctively knew that "forevermore" was what we had in mind.

I clearly recall a conversation with friends about wedding vows shortly after our marriage. They were also recently married and insisted that vows were not what kept their marriage together. If their relationship ever deteriorated, they would not stay together just because of those promises. I was suddenly faced with having to consider the true meaning of marriage.

At that moment it became clear to me that there has to be more to marriage than romantic feelings. If our marriage was to last for a lifetime, there had to be a decision and a commitment. There has to be a decision to love and a commitment to do whatever it takes from day to day to keep that love strong and to make life together work. To me the wedding vows Lani and I had spoken were a statement of that decision. When we did hit the inevitable bumps in the road, there would be no room to question our commitment. As we assumed that every problem had a solution, and as we worked through our problems together, our love did grow deeper.

It amazes me to look at this partnership in retrospect. Our separate paths from across the world somehow came together. The hundreds of separate decisions we made in our lives led us to a common point in time and place. We were different in about every way possible, but something attracted us to each other. Our relationship grew deeper and multilayered. We made a commitment, maintained a marriage, and built a family. Lani and I worked at this in a diligent and an intelligent manner, and I always felt we deserved our success. To some extent we could even consider ourselves the masters of our fate in the marriage sphere.

A DECISION TO LOVE

"If something is bothering you about our relationship, Lorraine, why don't you just spell it out."

Eric Teitelbaum[21]

However, there was also something mysterious about this process that makes it hard to take credit for it. At this point in the story, I hesitate to use the word *miraculous*, but at times something higher did seem to lead us along this journey.

> The point of philosophy is to start with something so simple as not to seem worth stating and to end with something so paradoxical that no one will believe it.
>
> —Bertrand Russell[22]

> **MBA**, n. Bearer of an academic credential untainted by the musty odor of great books, and therefore held in high esteem throughout the business world.[23]

CHAPTER FIVE

An Apostle of Maslow

You can't be a full-time husband, father, and Marine officer without a sense of purpose. There was a higher calling in each of these roles, and I often felt satisfaction from "duty well performed." This feeling was not constant, however, as I vacillated between confidence and doubt that I was doing all I should.

After Vietnam my self-confidence was not what it had been, and this had its consequences. If I were not the master of my fate, then who or what was? Even though I always considered myself a skeptical person, I also considered myself open to new facts and ideas—the kind of person I would call a seeker. This tendency became more pronounced as I continued my search for truths about life and my place in it.

In 1971 my Marine Corps career took another upward turn when I was selected for a program allowing me to finish graduate school at George Washington University. The Corps seemed to agree that I would be a more effective officer with a master's degree in business administration. After working through the core curriculum, I focused on psychology-based courses in individual, group, and organizational behavior. I found these topics professionally useful and personally stimulating. Could psychology even help me answer those bigger questions that were always in the back of my mind?

In response to this, Abraham Maslow seemed to say yes. Maslow was one of the most recognized psychologists of this era and chair of the Brandeis University psychology department. His unique contribution to psychology was the novel approach of studying the needs and behavior of *healthy* people. This was in sharp contrast to the widely used Freudian psychoanalytic approach focusing on the root causes of neurotic behavior.

In simplified form Maslow's theoretical structure holds that human beings are motivated by certain common drives that can be arranged in a hierarchical order. These include first the basic physiological needs, then the needs for safety, belongingness, esteem, and self-actualization. When the *lower* needs are satisfied to some extent, then the *higher* ones can become operative.[24] By studying very successful people, Maslow focused attention on the higher end of the spectrum and the process of self-actualization.

The idea here is that after we fill our more-basic needs, there remains a drive to find the peace that can only come from fulfilling our true nature. This piqued my interest. Who doesn't want to be self-actualized? By most measures I thought I was, but I knew there was room for a lot more inner peace in my life.

Among his self-actualized subjects, Maslow found frequent occurrences of mystical or "peak" experiences. These usually brought on convictions that profound things had happened and the recipients had been somehow transformed. Since he was an atheist, Maslow purposefully disassociated these experiences from the theological or supernatural realm.[25] He believed that most organized religions had lost the original visions of their founders and actually interfered with the abilities of their followers to experience their own authentic mystical experiences. I was inclined to agree with this observation.

Maslow's influence on my life was substantial in several ways. I relied on his theory of needs as the basis of my master's thesis, "Motivation of Enlisted Servicemen," and found his approach a useful way to look at human behavior and motivation. His theoretical structure guided much of the management literature of the time and affected my leadership style as a Marine officer and later as a businessman.

On a personal level, the idea of self-actualization stimulated a lot of thought and action. The search for some kind of peak experience seemed a new approach to my earlier attempts to directly experience God or some form of ultimate reality. This gave me a new mission: to find the one thing that would fulfill my nature and bring inner peace to my life. Unfortunately this proved to be a very elusive goal.

At this point in my career, the Marine Corps presented a problem. When I was promoted to major, one of my friends shook my hand and said, "Welcome to the ranks of middle management." It took a while for the meaning of this remark to sink in. After graduate school I found myself on Okinawa with the Third Marine Division and without Lani or my brand-new daughter, Anastasia. The separation was bad enough. At the same time, my military career took a definite turn into middle management.

Over the next several years, I was assigned various staff duties of a noncommand nature. This is not to say there weren't plenty of challenges. I deployed out of Okinawa as the executive officer, or second in command, of a battalion landing team—back to Vietnam waters. Fortunately I had a great commanding officer who was a superb troop leader and gave me plenty of room to function on my own. During a busy and productive deployment in Southeast Asian waters, I coordinated training for foreign Marine units from Vietnam and Taiwan. An especially productive tour on Taiwan culminated with porcelain chopsticks and too many toasts at a formal dinner with the commandant of the Nationalist Chinese Marine Corps.

Back in the States a year later, Lani, Anastasia, and I reunited and headed for California. For this stage of our family life, we purchased a little orange Volkswagen camper with a pop-up top. It cruised along pretty well on level ground but strained up the inclines. In its fixed position in a campground, it also had no air conditioning. As the climate got hotter, and I was the only one who could sleep, harmony began to suffer. As we approached our destination in the high desert, the vegetation went from sparse to nonexistent, and the morale of my little unit plummeted even further.

In this barren and inhospitable environment, Lani characteristically saw the bright side and quickly found her positive attitude. She proceeded to make a home in the Mohave Desert and have our first son, Bayliss. She made friends, built furniture, rode horses, and boycotted the Officers' Wives Club. When the General asked her about this, she stated that her job was to keep *her* Marine happy. Who could argue with that? Certainly not I and not even the general. Since those years out West, I have always considered Lani the perfect pioneer woman. With good humor and grit, she endured separations and took care of her husband and children under very tough conditions. She also went to California in a covered wagon.

Our final Marine Corps duty turned out to be at the place where it had started for me: The Citadel. My duties involved being a professor and an adviser to cadet units. This was mostly fun since I knew so much about cadet life from personal experience. This job, like the others I have characterized as middle management, had its unique challenges and rewards. It was especially exciting to see my Marine protégés progress through college and into their careers. It was similar to growing up with my own children. In both cases I could see something of myself going into the future. I was struck by the realization that this put me in touch with something of a lasting nature. I had never given much thought to life after death and had never been motivated by heavenly rewards, but I could grasp this concrete form of immortality.

As we neared twenty years of active military service, Lani and I considered the future. Even though I loved the Marine Corps, the decision to retire at that time was not difficult. Our third child, Catherine Alexa, was still an infant, and Anastasia was nearing ten years old. We had seen others endure a lot of family problems while moving from place to place with young children, especially teenagers. My next duty station would be another unaccompanied tour to Okinawa followed by the ultimate middle-management experience for a lieutenant colonel: Headquarters Marine Corps. With employment opportunities at The Citadel and business opportunities in Myrtle Beach, it seemed like the time to do something new.

The Marine Corps gave me a higher calling and sense of purpose at every stage of my career. God continued to be a remote and unapproachable figure whereas Marine esprit de corps was tangible and full of its own religious overtones. There was also growing purpose to my career as a husband and father. Whatever I did there was always the underlying mission to serve and defend my family and country. However, my sense of a high calling never seemed quite as clear and urgent as it had been when commanding a rifle company in combat. Over time the goal of finding that one thing to "fulfill my nature" seemed to slip further from my grasp. Instead I went through a gradual process of lowering my expectations. That process accelerated when I took off the uniform.

> **Congregation**, n. The subjects of an experiment in hypnotism.[26]

> **Conversion**, n. The act of submitting to religious doctrine, cured by regular church attendance.[27]

CHAPTER SIX

Going through the Episcopal Motions

Marines call civilian life the *outside*. Sometimes they long for it; sometimes they fear it. I had my own hopes and anxieties, both of which were fulfilled. I soon found new things to worry about and new challenges to confront. The demands of a small business in a busy resort town were totally new and absorbing.[28] For the first time, I had no chain of command going up and no higher echelon deciding my fate. There were only customers, employees, and creditors to keep happy and a bottom line to keep in the black. Gas shortages, hurricanes, ice storms, and lawsuits were there to remind me that I was never quite the master of my business's fate. Thankfully these usually proved negotiable bumps in the road. There seemed to be opportunities for growth and bright horizons ahead.

Community life was a new experience for Lani and me. For the first time, we felt we were building long-term relationships with friends and business associates. Schools, the chamber of commerce, banks, owners' associations, hospitals, and charities called for active service. We tried to be good community citizens by getting involved and doing our part.

As we considered our place in the bigger scheme of things, there was one base we did not cover for some time. That was church. This had to be considered because we were in South Carolina, generally conceded to be ground zero of the Bible Belt. Even so, this was one obligation I hoped we could ignore. We lived in a resort town, and were in a seven-day-a-week business. I reasoned we could go to different churches occasionally to keep up appearances while using most of our Sundays for rest, relaxation, and family time. If God cared at all, I thought, he would rather we enjoy his creation than spend time inside a building on uncomfortable seats.

Lani did not go for this plan. The problem was the kids. She had not had a strong church affiliation as a child and always felt shortchanged, like she was on the outside of something looking in. My childhood had been the flip side of that coin: I had been affiliated to the point that the Sundays of my youth seemed like jail time. Lani persisted in her belief that the children needed the sense of belonging a church could provide. Guess what we did.

Actually, by this time, Lani and I had worked out a pretty good arrangement for settling questions such as this and for general decision making in our family. I got to make all the big decisions. For instance, I decided who we would vote for in the presidential elections and what our foreign policy would be toward China and other important issues of that nature. She got to handle the smaller decisions, like what the family would do on any given day.

Although my background was Presbyterian, certain friends and relatives and a good youth program steered us into the local Episcopal Church. I gritted my teeth, read the services from the prayer book, sang the hymns by Bach, and did the kneeling thing. My family seemed happy with all this, but I felt like an enemy agent trying to maintain my cover. I kept a low profile by saying little and avoiding classes or groups with a lot of discussion. This did not seem difficult. In fact if I had gotten to know those around me better, I would have found out I was not so out of place. They don't call Episcopalians the "frozen chosen" for nothing.

My somewhat vaguely defined purpose at that time was to provide a service to the public and care for my family. The profit motive was not as exalted as defending my country, but after all that was why I had defended my country—to allow average people to lead normal lives and to do what I was now doing.

When I look back on this time, I feel I was quietly taking on my childhood pattern of "doing the right thing." A higher purpose was not an issue as long as there were new challenges to overcome. Even lacking more inspired motivations, I continued to have a strong sense of duty with a tendency to feel guilty over not doing enough. This had been a pretty good recipe for an effective student and Marine and seemed to work for a businessman and would-be community leader as well. To a lesser extent, it even made for a somewhat effective father and husband. I might have wondered more about how this structure would hold up during difficult times.

Being a pretty slow learner, it took me about ten years to find out. Over that time my first concern was the business. Hard work and many construction projects brought us to our size limit with staff increases and bigger budgets. We grew with the rest of the economy. Fortunately the income grew as well, although we were putting a lot of it back into the company.

As time went by, however, something of a routine started to establish itself. Little by little, problems I had once solved popped back up. Employee turnover, customer complaints, tax increases, weather crises, local government issues, and the myriad other problems of small business seemed to have second lives, never remaining solved for long. I found that doing the right thing over and over was not so easy. As my efficiency declined, I learned to live with even more anxiety. I had never thought before about the "treadmill" of life, but I began to be conscious of circular patterns in my activity.

Our fourth child, Windom, was born in 1984, and before we knew it we had a two-year-old and a teenager in the same house. The two middle kids were running for cover, and the crying came in stereo. Lani was walking the fine line of sanity, and I was looking for any kind of problem to solve at work. Fortunately our family Richter scale peaked during this period, although aftershocks continued. As the other kids worked their way up the teen ladder, we encountered plenty of challenges. Thanks to Lani our family unit grew stronger through every trial. My role as ultimate disciplinarian was tested and *usually* respected. For the most part, I just kept on working hard, especially during the summer months that most consider family time. I usually had the feeling I wasn't doing enough.

The death of parents brings each of us to another stage of life for which we are never ready. My father's death was unexpected. He was seventy-two, retired, and still going strong at golf and yachting. I blamed it on my military service that I'd never quite gotten around to knowing him as a person. I could and should have tried harder. There were many things left unsaid, including a simple "I love you."

Another tragedy in our family was the death of Lani's mother. Eleanor Hillwig was a uniquely intelligent and caring woman and found one of her greatest roles in life as grandmother to our children. Every time she was with us, each of them seemed to grow intellectually in some new direction. Her death was a blow to the kids that neither Lani nor I was capable of explaining. It was also a blow to Lani with dire consequences.

There is an old expression that says, "If Mama's happy then everybody's happy." It would follow that if Mama is depressed…well, you know the rest. The light of our family went dim for a long time. Before her mother died, Lani had allowed few days to go by without debriefing her either in person or by telephone. In fact she often felt her joys were not even real until she was able to share them with her mother. Without this touchstone she kept on functioning, but something was missing. Unfortunately I had nothing to say that could relieve her pain. Over the months, as her sadness grew, a tumor grew with it. We followed her along this descending path to a very low point and a bout with surgery. I'm not proud to say I was never fully conscious of how bad things were for Lani or our family for much of that time.

My mother suffered for years with emphysema, especially near the end. Her death brought relief with the sadness. It also brought the realization that there was no longer anyone out there in front of me in this life. I had never thought about the comfort of having another generation out there. Without it there was suddenly a void with nothing between me and the end of my own life. This was unknown territory I had never before considered.

As a young Marine involved in a lot of dangerous activities, I'd had a pretty blasé attitude about death. This had shifted a little when a friend told me a story from his hospital bed in Vietnam. His unit had been caught in the open by enemy fire, and he had been wounded badly. After crawling for what seemed like forever, he was bleeding, thirsty, and in shock. He thought, *Well, this is it. I'm not going to make it.* Then another shell hit in front of him, kicking dirt in his face. With that he said, "Dammit, I'm not going to die here!" He crawled on and lived to tell the story. I never came face to face with death in quite that manner, but I was moved by this friend's testimony that most of us will fight to live even in the direst circumstance.

I had thought a lot more about death as I saw it up close for myself and lost friends on other battlefields. I thought a lot about it again with the passing of parents and other relatives. No matter what you believe, death is an ominous presence in life. A poet said, "Death has a thousand doors to let out life."[29] This is an especially bleak prospect for those of us who consider ourselves skeptics and masters of our fate.

> **Stress**, n. An effective antidote to the increased life expectancy made possible by recent advances in medical science.[30]

> **Angst**, n. A form of suffering caused by too much thinking.[31]

CHAPTER SEVEN

Hard Times for a Skeptic

I tried to treat my fiftieth birthday like any other. Unfortunately, at the half-century mark, you can't avoid the fact that your life is more than half gone even if you're healthy and lucky. It is definitely a time for reflection, as if I ever needed more of that. I had been frustrated over and over during my life while trying to grasp the bigger picture. It was really disturbing to realize the bigger picture might be getting more important.

By all outward indications, I was having a good life. I had a beautiful wife, healthy children, successful business, nice home, two cars, and a good reputation. I was in better than average health and had no drinking, smoking, drug, or mental problems of which I was aware. I was in love with Lani and never had any doubt she loved me in return. The fact that I worried a lot sometimes seemed pretty ridiculous even to me.

Over the years, however, the subsurface of my life seemed to follow its own down-trending trajectory. Even though there was little outward evidence of it, the negatives already described built up—a lack of control over random events, declining excitement about work, money worries, deaths, and family crises. I ran across the definition of a midlife crisis as being a time of profound psychological turbulence that usually occurs between the ages of thirty-eight and fifty-five. I don't like the idea of an important part of my life being defined by a cliché, but this was definitely a time of internal turbulence.

Whether or not my experience fits into a definition of anything, I see now that I gradually entered a period of my life where the color was draining away. Even though the exterior seemed fine, my spirit of excitement and adventure imperceptibly dwindled. It was like the classic example of the frog's demise: If you drop him in a pot of hot water, he will jump out. Instead, drop him in cold water and turn up the heat gradually, and he will soon be cooked. I was the frog who didn't even know he had a problem. The challenges just faded. Life became mostly a matter of keeping my little herd of sheep (business problems, civic duties, family responsibilities, etc.) going down the road with a certain amount of order and direction.

It took a long time for me to figure out that something was lacking in my life. Even though I had a lot to do, I came to see I was living a life without purpose. That unpleasant reality check from Vietnam kept coming back to haunt me. If I were not the master of my fate or the captain of my soul then who or what was?

As I pondered this question, I kept remembering a comedian from the past who exhorted his audiences, "Don't tell me your doubts. I've got doubts of my own. Tell me what you *believe* in!"[32] As a skeptic I was always able to explain my doubts eloquently. However, I gradually became aware of the fact that I had nothing to say on the positive side.

My answer to this problem, as has been the case all my life, was to seek more information. As my so-called church life went on in its superficial way, I stepped up my efforts in a wide range of areas. My interest in philosophy grew stronger and led me into other fields: anthropology, physics, and cosmology. I found books like Fritjof Capra's *The Tao of Physics* intriguing. His attempts to correlate Eastern religions with developments in modern physics struck a chord. He tried to describe an underlying unity that could be found in the quantum nature of matter and the deeper realms of consciousness in mysticism. He observed that this reality is almost impossible to express in ordinary language. This type of discourse was always appealing to me even though it ultimately seemed to lead nowhere.

Still I continued to plow ahead, seeking to garner ever more information about cosmology, evolution, the origins and nature of human beings, and comparative religions. I tried to keep an open mind during my pursuit of such knowledge but have to admit I was often testing the tenets of my childhood faith against what I was learning. I was also attending church on a somewhat regular basis and subjecting myself to certain religious interpretations of this information. I was a skeptic but, I admit, one with a lot of ancestral religious baggage.

So far I have presented my journey in a more or less chronological order. However, at this point I would like to share with my skeptical reader some of the information I gathered over a period of years as I searched to understand the important questions about the meaning of life and my purpose in living it. Some of this information and my conclusions based on it are the subjects of the next sections of this book. I have organized them by subject without regard to time sequence or importance. Part two will deal with issues related to science, part three with the Bible, and part four with the difficult questions that were always important to me as a skeptic.

PART TWO

A Side Journey into Science

> **Deist**, n. One who believes in God but reserves the right to worship the Devil.[33]

> Science without religion is lame, religion without science is blind.
> —Albert Einstein[34]

CHAPTER EIGHT

The Watchmaker God

Our first demand as skeptics is proof of God's existence. From an early age, I was unable to find convincing, independent verification outside the church that there was a god, especially one interested in me as an individual human being. As I ventured farther from my hometown support system, more and more of the outside world seemed to reinforce this skepticism.

High school and college biology left me with the general understanding that life started in the primordial ocean, that a simple life form emerged onto land, that the evolutionary process caused ever more complex organisms to appear, and that the process of natural selection then took over to govern the fate of living things. This widely taught and widely held view of the world reinforced my skepticism toward the Bible and organized religion in general. If there were a god, he had to be a remote figure that may have started the world but then had no involvement in it.

Gradually I came to realize the extent to which many scientists and academicians use these commonly held scientific opinions to argue against even the existence of God and any supernatural force in the creation of the universe or life. These *scientific* views have been extremely influential and have gradually been absorbed into the general consciousness of the public.

This has had an obvious impact on attitudes toward religion. The Bureau of Census has reported that those who consider themselves atheist or nonreligious have grown from 1 percent of the population to 9 percent over the past hundred years.[35] This small percentage increase represents many millions of individual human beings. I can assert from my experience that there are even more who consider themselves religious but are still uncertain or doubtful about God.

The concept of a "watchmaker" god who started it all a long time ago has been an appealing concept to many skeptics through the ages. The more I thought about it, however, the more illogical it seemed. If God is no longer involved in the world, there might as well be no god. And how logical is it to conceive of a god capable of starting it all but incapable of influencing it? Or if he were willing to start it, why would he be unwilling to be involved with it? Belief in the watchmaker god may be a fallback position for someone who can't explain certain mysteries about the natural world, but unfortunately, for a thoughtful skeptic, it is a dead-end street. I needed to decide whether there was a *real* god or not. If there was then I might have to reconsider what he is capable of doing.

In the following pages, I will discuss several areas of science that have had distinct impacts on my own religious belief and the beliefs of the general public. I affirm the fact that I am not a scientist or a theologian and speak only as an ordinary person seeking the truth about important questions. I hope my skeptical readers will test some of their own beliefs that have been influenced by modern science.

> My theology, briefly, is that the universe was dictated but not signed.
> —Christopher Morley[36]

> The advance of scientific knowledge does not seem to make either our universe or our inner life in it any less mysterious.
> —J. B. S. Haldane[37]

CHAPTER NINE
Why Are So Many Physicists Believers?

Cosmology is the scientific discipline devoted to the study of the universe. The question of whether or not there was a beginning has traditionally been a critical issue. If there were a definite beginning, it would follow logically that there was a cause. This idea opens the door for speculation about a creation and a creator, both subjects that many scientists would rather avoid. The "steady state" model, holding that the universe has existed throughout eternity, made this a moot point until mounting evidence disproved it in the 1960s.

The static universe first came into question in 1915 with Albert Einstein's general theory of relativity. When his equations seemed to show that the universe should be either contracting or expanding, Einstein injected a cosmological constant, or fudge factor, to hold it steady. He would not entertain the idea of a universe expanding from a point that could not be explained by physics. He later described this as "the biggest blunder of my life."[38]

Using Einstein's equations without the cosmological factor, other scientists projected models of an expanding universe. From 1968 to 1970, Steven Hawking and others demonstrated that the equations of general relativity prove there is a boundary of space and time at some point in the past, which they termed a *singularity*. Hawking was also uncomfortable with the implications of such an origin; he stated, "Under such conditions, all the known laws of science would break down. This is a disaster for science."[39]

The concept of the sudden appearance of the universe has become affectionately known as the Big Bang. At first it was a mathematical model, and astronomers and physicists have consistently provided proof of its validity through observation and experiment. From the point of view of basic physics, the model provided the first explanation for the creation of the lightest elements, hydrogen and helium (which together comprise over 99 percent of all matter in the universe). The other heavier elements have been shown to come from the nuclear processes within stars. However, creation of the light elements required an intense heat many magnitudes greater than anything known. Only the Big Bang could account for these elements.[40]

In 1965 Arno Penzias and Robert Wilson of Bell Laboratories documented the microwave background radiation in the universe, confirming a key prediction of the Big Bang model. By 1977 the renowned physicist and Nobel Prize-winner Steven Weinberg was calling it the standard model even though he did not consider it the "most satisfying theory imaginable of the origin of the universe."[42] As an outspoken atheist, he found it difficult to live with the "embarrassing vagueness about the very beginning."[43]

George Smoot and a Lawrence Berkeley Laboratory team working with the NASA cosmic background explorer (COBE) satellite practically eliminated all doubt about the standard model in 1992. Their careful measurements of variations in cosmic background radiation explained the early formations of the stars, galaxies, and other structures in the

WHY ARE SO MANY PHYSICISTS BELIEVERS?

universe. This data answered one of the last and biggest questions about the validity of the Big Bang. In explaining these results to the press, Smoot made the comment, "If you're religious, it's like seeing God."[44] In 2006 he received the Nobel Prize in Physics for his work that "provided increased support for the Big Bang scenario for the origin of the universe."[45]

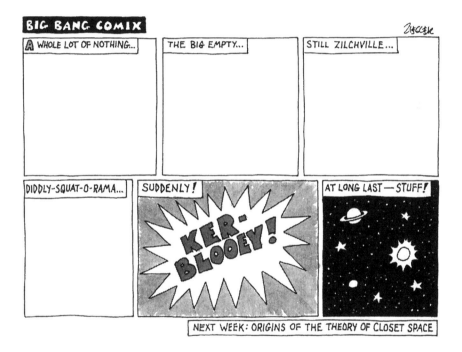

Jack Ziegler[41]

The fact that this theory has moved from consensus to near-unanimous acceptance among cosmologists does not prove the existence of God. It does, however, bring us to the fact of a beginning to the universe and should lead to speculation about a first cause. George Smoot expressed confidence that science would eventually be able to explain everything back to this starting point. However, he went on to say:

> *Go back further still, beyond the moment of creation—what then? What was there before the Big Bang? What was there before time began? Facing this, the ultimate question challenges our faith in the power of science to find explanations of nature. The existence of a singularity—in this case the given, unique state from which the universe emerged—is anathema to science because it is beyond explanation. There can be no answer to why such a state existed. Is this, then, where scientific explanation breaks down and God takes over, the artificer of that singularity, that initial simplicity?*[46]

The evidence for the beginning of the universe points to a first cause that cosmology cannot explain. If a scientific explanation is beyond the reach of science, there is no way to rule out the possibility of another explanation, such as the existence of a creator.

There are experts in cosmology who not only consider the idea of a creator feasible but find amazing parallels with the creation account of the Bible. Arno Penzias, mentioned above, received the Nobel Prize in Physics in 1978. In *The New York Times* on March 12, 1987, he stated, "The best data we have (concerning the Big Bang) are exactly what I would have predicted, had I nothing to go on but the five books of Moses, the Psalms, the Bible as a whole."[47] George Smoot made the statement, albeit reluctantly, that "there is no doubt that a parallel exists between the Big Bang as an event and the Christian notion of creation from nothing."[48]

Looking at cosmology from another perspective, I discovered an accumulation of data in recent decades pointing to the remarkable degree of fine-tuning in the physical parameters of the universe. This data points to the conclusion that our universe was no cosmological accident. Martin Rees, professor of astronomy at Cambridge and named Astronomer Royal by the queen in 1995,

WHY ARE SO MANY PHYSICISTS BELIEVERS?

has written about the six numbers that underlie the physical properties of the universe. He stated that if any one of them were altered "even to the tiniest degree, there would be no stars, no complex elements, no life."[49] Robert Jastrow, an astronomer and self-described agnostic, addressed the critical density of matter and the fact that a variation one second after the Big Bang of more or less than one part in one million would have precluded the formation of the universe. George Smoot cites examples of what has been termed the *anthropic principle*:

> *If the strong nuclear force had been slightly weaker, the universe would have been composed of hydrogen only—slightly stronger—and all the hydrogen would have been converted to helium. Slight variation in the excess of protons over antiprotons—one billion and one to one billion—might have produced a universe with no baryonic matter or a cataclysmic plentitude of it. Had the expansion rate of the universe one second after the Big Bang been smaller by one part in a hundred thousand trillion, the universe would have recollapsed long ago. An expansion more rapid by one part in a million would have excluded the formation of stars and planets.*[50]

Not only is each of these fundamental parameters highly improbable, but they are all improbable *independently* of each other. Taken together they comprise a practically statistical impossibility that the universe came into existence by chance. To explain this phenomenon, some scientists have postulated the existence of trillions of other universes, making the extreme improbability of this one more likely. Some assert we are stuck with the brute fact of a chance universe no matter how improbable the odds.

Some scientists, however, admit the possibility of a simpler answer. Considering these fundamental laws of the universe, the famous and very nonreligious physicist and science writer Paul Davies observed there is "circumstantial evidence for something deeper," there is "the appearance of design," and "something like meaning or purpose, or at least rationality, surely lies behind it all."[51] Reflecting this idea, physicist Richard Feynman observed, "The fact that there are rules at all to be checked is a kind of miracle; that it is possible to find a rule, like the inverse square law of gravitation, is some sort of miracle."[52] In his best-selling book *A Brief History of Time,* Stephen Hawking said it even more plainly: "It would be very difficult to explain why the universe should have begun in just this way, except as the act of a God who intended to create beings like us."[53]

Another great physicist, Roger Penrose, wrote about the beauty of mathematics, considering whether pure mathematics is a process of invention or discovery. He believed that in many cases, he was "uncovering truths, which are, in fact, already 'there'—truths whose existence is quite independent of the mathematicians' activities." He further concluded, "One may take the view that in such cases, the mathematicians have stumbled upon 'works of God.'"[54]

In my study of cosmology, I began to see a pattern. One well-known scientist said, "If we need an atheist for a debate, we go to the philosophy department. The physics department isn't much use."[55] Physicists seem to have a clear picture of what they do and do not know. To the extent that they understand the universe, they see order and beauty. Many concede there may be mysteries beyond their understanding. Within this sphere of science, there seems to be some room for belief in an intelligent design and even a designer. For the other side of the debate, I had to look only behind most doors in the biology department to find someone ready and eager to argue against such a nonscientific concept as intelligent design.

> **Evolution**, n. A biological relay race hurtling onward and occasionally upward from the ancient muck, as trilobites and pterodactyls pass the baton to aardvarks and claims adjusters.[56]

CHAPTER TEN

Why Are So Many Biologists Atheists?

Just as the physical world at one time seemed to exist in a steady state, the many species of animal and plant life on Earth once seemed to be unchanging. No one knew precisely when or how life and the multitudinous forms of it came into existence. For centuries the biblical account of Genesis satisfied many and prevailed generally in the consciousness of much of Western civilization: "God made the wild animals according to their kinds, the livestock according to their kinds, and all the creatures that move along the ground according to their kinds."[57]

Charles Darwin was not the first to question how the species were created, but he is by far the best known. His book, *On the Origin of Species*, was published in 1859, culminating years of biological research and observation. He saw firsthand the tremendous variations among plants and animals even within species. He also observed that all plants and animals struggle to survive. He concluded that the process of struggle accounts for biological change in that certain variations are selected when they prove beneficial to survival and more successful in reproduction over time. His resulting theory proposed that all the species came into existence by a process of gradual, evolutionary change by which one species branched into others. The mechanism for this change was termed *natural selection*.

The simplicity of Darwin's thesis belies its scope and implications. It has become not only the organizing principle of biology but the intellectual foundation of much of science. His ideas and assumptions have influenced the thinking of scientists ever since they were published. Biologist Richard Dawkins observed that living organisms existed on Earth without knowing why for three thousand million years before "the truth finally dawned on one of them. His name was Charles Darwin."[58]

Darwin's work was interesting to scientists of his and our times and became widely known to the general public. Curiosity was intense from the beginning in this body of work, which seemed to explain the very process of life. The implications for religion were obvious. If this so-called evolution of living forms was a natural occurrence, what was the role of God? For many there was no longer any role. Richard Dawkins spoke for many when he said, "Darwin made it possible to be an intellectually fulfilled atheist."[59]

Sam Gross[60]

The history of opposition to Darwin's ideas is extensive. Creationism originated as a defense against the literal interpretation of the creation account in the book of Genesis. By using biblical authority to insist the Earth is fewer than ten thousand years old, creationists incurred the scorn of practically all within the scientific and academic communities. Gradually, more-thoughtful challenges to evolution have come from the fields loosely described as creation science and intelligent design. Most scientists and academicians continue to frame *any* challenge to evolution as superstition versus science.

The 1925 Scopes Trial was the earliest and most public conflict over evolution in the United States, capturing imaginations of that time and of later generations. To head off state legislation curtailing the teaching of evolution, the American Civil Liberties Union persuaded John Scopes, a Tennessee high school biology teacher, to participate in a legal challenge to a Tennessee statute making it unlawful "to teach any theory that denies the story of the Divine Creation of man."[61]

Public interest and two famous lawyers ensured the trial would be a media sensation. Three-time presidential candidate William Jennings Bryan prosecuted the case against Scopes, and the famous Clarence Darrow provided the defense. The story has lived on by means of stage, cinema, and television since then.

The most-enduring images of the trial come from the 1960 Hollywood production *Inherit the Wind.* In the movie version, the white-haired, jovial Spencer Tracey played Clarence Darrow. The bald, dark, and sinister Frederic March played the part of William Jennings Bryan. During the scene of the famous cross-examination on the seventh day of the trial, March, as Bryan, was portrayed as an unbending biblical literalist finally brought to a state of blathering incoherence by Darrow's artful reasonableness. On stage and screen, the reasoned approach of scientific evolution continues to triumph over the apparently dark and superstitious forces of our religious past.

To my amazement I found that the details of the trial revealed a completely different picture. During the cross-examination Darrow called Bryan to the stand as an expert witness on the Bible. The transcripts of the two-hour discussion show that Bryan more than held his own during the intense questioning. As Darrow tried to pin him down on the literal interpretation of Genesis, March said:

> *It would be just as easy for the kind of God we believe in to make the earth in six days as in six years or in six million years or in six hundred million years.*[62]

The trial turned out to be inconclusive. Mr. Scopes was convicted as charged, although the conviction was later thrown out on a technicality. Still, the event lives on in the media as a triumph of modern science over religious superstition.

There were, of course, some dark times in Western history when science did truly struggle to survive against a dogmatic religious establishment. Copernicus, Galileo, Newton, and even Darwin were attacked for their heresies against the Bible and church. In more-modern times, creationists, creation scientists, and advocates of intelligent design have weighed in against either evolution or the exclusivity of evolutionary theory in the educational system. With good reason scientists have fought for the independence of scientific inquiry from religious oversight.

I think it is clear that in the present day, science has won this war. The shoe is now on the other foot. Not only does science have freedom of inquiry, but religion is challenged in all areas to prove its relevance. Occasional school-board conflicts flare up but go nowhere in a broad sense. Scientists not only dominate the evolution debate but many, especially biologists, now freely apply the materialistic assumptions of the scientific approach to broader interpretations of life.

WHY ARE SO MANY BIOLOGISTS ATHEISTS?

These attitudes have gradually achieved wide acceptance. A biology text of the 1970s cites one of the predominant themes of modern thought as "the interpretability of natural events without recourse to an ultimate design or purpose," leading to a view of humanity that rules out any spiritual component. "Within man alone reside whatever aims and purposes there may be."[63] A more modern biology text asserts, "One of the fundamental principles of science is that Earthly phenomena are produced by natural, Earthly causes."[64]

Today this view is widespread among scientists and academics and prevails, to some extent, within the population at large. As I have already mentioned, the assumptions of the evolutionary doctrine colored my attitudes toward God and religion for many years. I have gradually become aware, however, that science may not have all the answers. Because there are things in the world we cannot study scientifically, it does not follow that such things are not real. Physicist Richard Feynman points out that:

> *Scientists take all those things that can be analyzed by observation, and thus the things called science are found out. But there are some things left out, for which the method does not work. This does not mean that those things are unimportant. They are, in fact, in many ways the most important.*[65]

It is not a criticism of science to say there are many things science has not yet explained. In the textbook cited above, there are numerous references to unanswered questions in evolutionary biology. Concerning the origin of life, there is "no interpretable record."[66] In summarizing the geological record of the Cambrian period, the writers conclude that "one of the major puzzles of the history of life as seen in the fossil record is this apparently sudden development of a diversity of advanced animals."[67] The book also explores contradictions between the concept of natural selection and the existence of altruism, concluding, "This question has not as yet been answered to the satisfaction of everyone."[68] Self-consciousness is cited as the unique trait of man, distinguishing him from all other animals. How this trait evolved is "necessarily speculative."[69]

The textbook puts forth each of these questions confidently, as a challenge that evolutionary biology will eventually solve. This is stated as a matter of fact based on an unshakeable view of the world and belief that everything has a natural cause that either has been or will be explained by the scientific method. I have a great respect for science and the progress made by scientists in understanding the natural world. The study of evolution has contributed much to this understanding. The scientific method rightfully focuses on natural causes and explanations. In their fields of study, scientists assume they will find natural causes for whatever is unknown. As I continued to explore this issue, I kept returning to two questions: Is this basic assumption of modern science truly scientific? And is there a natural cause for *everything*?

> **DNA**, n. A complex organic molecule characterized as the building block of life and appropriately shaped like a spiral staircase to nowhere.[70]

> **Y-Chromosome**, n. A line of genes designed for men only; the cause of virility, baldness, hockey, sex crimes, clever inventions and a disinclination to ask for directions when lost.[71]

CHAPTER ELEVEN
What about the Information?

Charles Darwin challenged the biblical view of the natural world by proposing that the species evolved gradually over long periods of time. Ironically Darwin never addressed the question of the origin of life. In the first edition of *On the Origin of Species*, he stated:

> *I should infer from analogy that probably all the organic beings that have ever lived on this earth have descended from some primordial form into which life was first breathed.*[72]

Darwin preferred to leave at least this space in the natural order for *past* divine intervention.

We have to fast-forward to the 1950s for the first serious effort to eliminate this "mystery" of the evolutionary process. Stanley Miller and Harold Urey at the University of Chicago attempted to show how life had first formed from chemical processes. To do this they created their approximation of the primordial atmosphere by combining water vapor, ammonia, methane, and hydrogen. Into this mixture they introduced electrical charges to simulate lightning. In the resulting solution, they found traces of amino acids. Since amino acids are known to be the basic components of proteins, the experiment was heralded as scientific proof of how the "building blocks of life" were first formed. Media and academic acceptance of these experiments gave them immediate and continuing textbook credibility.

Further investigation into this subject led in later years to other scientific voices' challenging Miller and Urey, but they garnered little commensurate attention. According to other scientists, the composition of the early Earth's atmosphere remains unknown and subject to conjecture. Miller and Urey assumed a natural chemical process in the origin of life and therefore used ingredients likely to produce organic molecules. They assumed free oxygen had been virtually absent from the primitive atmosphere since organic compounds decompose in its presence. This issue has not been resolved scientifically.[73] Dean Kenyon, professor of biology at San Francisco State University and a Stanford University biophysicist, wrote:

> *If one wishes to know whether a chemical evolutionary origin of life could have taken place, one cannot simply assume that it did take place and then argue that conditions on the prebiotic earth must have been such as to allow it to occur.*[74]

More-recent studies by the National Aeronautics and Space Administration also concluded, "Earth's atmospheric composition at the time of the origin of life is not known."[75] As scientists have wrestled with the problem of early amino acid and protein formation, some have even turned to outer space for an answer. A recent paper published in an Australian scientific journal stated:

> *Meteorites contain various organic molecules and amino acids, which are the precursors to protein molecules. Some researchers even proposed that asteroid and comet impacts could have delivered these "bricks of life" to Earth.*[76]

If true, this may answer one question but raises another: from where did the organic molecules on those meteorites come?

Beyond the issue of how the first amino acids were formed, the larger question has to do with the significance of those amino acids, whether created in a test tube, formed in the actual primordial atmosphere, or delivered from outer space. Could they assemble themselves into proteins, and could such proteins organize themselves into functioning cells? Modern cell biology and decades of research have not answered these questions, but they have provided a vast amount of new knowledge on the subject.

We know that the cell is the simplest life form and can exist either as a self-sustaining entity, like an amoeba, or as a component of a complex organism, such as a plant or animal. It is estimated the human body consists of twenty to thirty trillion cells of such microscopic size that about ten thousand would fit on the head of a pin. Although varied in function, all cells have certain processes in common: they live, consume nutrients, expel waste, reproduce, and eventually die.

Proteins are the building blocks of the cell and are formed by complex combinations of amino acids. Structural proteins make up the frameworks of the many different types of cells, tissues, and organs of the body. Specialized proteins called enzymes guide the biochemical reactions within the cell while other proteins function as antibodies, hormones, neurotransmitters, and transporters within the body. These are all large, complex molecules with molecular weights (the sum of the atomic weights within the molecule) from several thousand to more than a million. In comparison the molecular weight of a water molecule is eighteen. The three-dimensional shape of each protein gives it a unique fit with other molecules within the cell to catalyze a specific reaction or to build a specific structure. In other words they are not interchangeable. The human body contains more than thirty thousand different proteins, only a fraction of which we have analyzed and described chemically.

It has been calculated that the statistical probability of one simple protein molecule with a length of one hundred amino acids assembling at random is one chance in ten to the sixty-fifth power. This is a very small number and considered by statisticians to be even "vanishingly" small. When we consider the probability of more-complex proteins assembling themselves and then organizing to carry out the complex cell functions necessary for life, the number becomes so infinitesimal that some statisticians believe it exhausts the probabilistic possibilities of a four-billion-year-old Earth or even a ten-billion-year-old universe.[77] Chance is not an adequate explanation for this amount of organized complexity.

Since Watson and Crick's pioneering work with DNA in the 1950s, we have had a better understanding of the process of protein formation and coordination of the complex functions within the cell. It is all accomplished under the control of the cell's DNA (deoxyribonucleic acid) residing in long chains of molecules formed into the well-known double helix structure. The basic units, or alphabet, of the DNA chain are four base molecules (chemically referred to as *A*, *T*, *G*, and *C*). These combine in certain ways to form nucleotides or base pairs.

A group of three base pairs, or a codon, specifies one amino acid. A group of codons, referred to as a gene, specifies a sequence of amino acids to produce one protein. The complex, chainlike protein molecule may contain from fifty to several hundred amino acid subunits arranged in a precise, three-dimensional order. Each gene specifies both which amino acids are needed and the sequence of their combination to produce a protein. Signals to activate specific genes for protein production pass into the cell nucleus as often as ten times per second.

Each cell of every organism contains a complete set of DNA that enables it to carry out its intended functions and to reproduce. Each strand within humans contains more than three billion base pairs organized into more than thirty thousand genes. The DNA within a human cell would measure three meters in length if stretched out, and all the DNA in the body would stretch across the solar system.[78]

"*Your DNA doesn't match your credit history.*"

Peter C. Vey[79]

The properties and components of DNA are amazingly complex, and scientists are still exploring them intensely. What is apparent even to the nonexpert, however, is the underlying fact that DNA is in every way *information*. Just as letters form words and words sentences, the base pairs of DNA form amino acids, and amino acids form proteins. But just as letters don't spontaneously form themselves into words, neither do amino acids just randomly become proteins. They have to be sequenced carefully and intricately through a process of applied information.

To continue the alphabet analogy, one organism's complete DNA code is more than a sentence or a paragraph. It is even more than a book. DNA is more like a library of information. Science does not explain how this or any amount of information can be spontaneously assembled and organized. Professors Miller and Urey found a few metaphorical Scrabble tiles at the bottom of their test tube. The existence of those "letters" does not explain the Library of Congress.

At the DNA level, the quest to explain the origin of life is confronted by an apparent paradox. DNA stores information to produce proteins and to replicate itself. Proteins are needed to interpret genetic information but are also the product of this interpretation. Biologists continue to speculate on which could have come first—DNA or functioning proteins. And how could either have come into existence without the other? To explain the origin of life, science would have to explain the origin of amino acid and protein sequencing and the organization of proteins into cells, tissues, and organs. In other words from where did the *information* come? So far there is no scientific answer to this question.

Equally baffling is the question of how the first DNA molecules reproduced themselves. Of necessity, scientists have focused for decades on this question of early DNA replication. In other words once started, how did the process continue? Dr. Charles Carter of the University of North Carolina recently published a paper examining the various known approaches to the question and concluded:

WHAT ABOUT THE INFORMATION?

> *The study leaves open the question of exactly how those primitive systems managed to replicate themselves—something neither the RNA World hypothesis nor the Peptide-RNA World theory can yet explain.*[80]

As he ruled out any known answer to the question, he continues his search in other areas.

Other origin-of-life biologists also continue to seek answers and new knowledge about DNA and the beginning of life. This quest animates their professional lives and promises to increase our understanding of the cellular processes that support and even define life. These biologists may not have all the answers now, but they have confidence that all will be uncovered eventually.

As I thought about this scientific confidence, it occurred to me that I was seeing similarities to what a religious person might call faith. This scientific faith rests in the belief that there is a natural cause for everything. However, it takes a true leap of faith to believe that a chemical determinant will be found to explain either the spontaneous assembly of protein molecules or the vast information content of DNA. Such faith may eventually be rewarded. So far, however, I am led to the conclusion that faith in an intelligent designer is not only reasonable but probably *more* reasonable than a belief in random chance or chemical necessity.

> **Man**, n. An animal so lost in rapturous contemplation of what he thinks he is as to overlook what he indubitably ought to be.[81]

> It is even harder for the average ape to believe that he has descended from man.
> —H. L. Mencken[82]

CHAPTER TWELVE

The *Evolution* of Human Beings

Unless God made the world ten thousand years ago in such a way that it would look older than it is today, geologists have apparently proven the Earth to be four and a half to five billion years old. Scientists found the earliest evidence of life in the 3.8-billion-year-old Greenland rock, and the oldest fossils of algae-like organisms, estimated to be 3.5 billion years old.[83] For about two billion years, life continued on our young planet in microscopic single-celled forms. Fossils of more-complex organisms, such as sponges, jellyfish, and worms, have been dated to the Late Precambrian period, about 650 million years ago.[84]

Over the next thirty million years or so of the Cambrian period, all the phyla representing the animal kingdom of today came into existence, as documented by an extensive fossil record from that period found near Cambria, Wales, in the 1800s. This rapid advance in the evolutionary process has been referred to as the "Cambrian Explosion."[85] Many advocates of creation science argue thirty million years is not enough time for the expected evolutionary process to unfold. Even evolutionists seem to agree it is at least an apparent departure from Darwin's requirement that,

> *As natural selection acts solely by accumulating slight, successive, favorable variations, it can produce no great or sudden modifications; it can act only by short and slow steps.*[86]

To some Darwin's slow, methodical branching process is not compatible with the phenomenon of the Cambrian Explosion.

Biologists have also had to rely on a lot of speculation about the origin of the larger and more-complex phyla of the Cambrian period due to the lack of fossil evidence showing how the transitions occurred. The following excerpt from an older biology text is illustrative:

> *Once they were established, the metazoans (multi-cellular animals with cells forming tissues and organs) left a fossil record, which allows interpretations of their evolutionary history. The record of origin, however, is just the opposite. It poses many problems, most of which cannot be answered without considerable speculation.*[87]

There has been extensive debate over the adequacy of the fossil record in general toward proving the transitions between species. Well-known Harvard writer and evolutionist Stephen J. Gould made the famous statement, "The extreme rarity of transitional forms in the fossil record persists as the trade secret of paleontology."[88] To cope with this problem, he developed his theory of punctuated equilibrium, (or "punk eek" in academia) to show how evolution could have occurred in spurts with little fossil evidence of the process. David Kitts, a well-known geologist and professor of science history, has said:

> *Despite the bright promise that paleontology provides a means of "seeing" evolution, it has presented some nasty difficulties for evolutionists, the most notorious of which is the presence of "gaps" in the fossil record. Evolution requires intermediate forms between species and paleontology does not provide them.*[89]

Even as skeptics of evolution point out these shortcomings, I believe that most generally concede the effectiveness of evolutionary theory in explaining the changes that have occurred *within* species over the span of natural history. Creation science has coined the terms *microevolution* and *macroevolution* to make the distinction between change within species and the change of one species into another. The purpose of this is to concede natural processes at the *lower* level while attributing action at the *higher* level to God.

I can see no practical purpose for this distinction. If there is a God, he would have been the architect of the evolutionary process and could obviously have acted in many ways to influence it. With such a complex and efficient system, he would have had no need to intervene in the process very often. His interventions would probably have been subtle. In some cases, they could have been more overt or even catastrophic (such as an extinction event). If there is no God, then the distinction between macroevolution and microevolution is even more irrelevant.

The most important case of macroevolution (to use the term one more time) is, of course, the evolution of human beings. That an evolutionary process occurred is a fundamental and practically nondebatable tenet of modern science. I am not qualified to debate it either in a general sense. However, there are a few particulars that seem worthy of consideration.

Paleontologists estimate that mankind's evolutionary process started as early as ten million years ago, when the hominids (considered to be those destined to become humans) and pongids (the line of modern apes) took divergent paths.[90] Up until several decades ago, most scientists and textbook writers viewed hominid evolution as a long series of improvements during which an early species of apelike creatures gradually changed to others with new anatomical and behavioral features and ultimately became what we know as modern man, or the species *Homo sapiens*. This simplified view of human evolution had to give way to a new understanding with the advent of modern genetics.

In 1999 a group of scientists published a paper in the Oxford *Journal of Molecular Biology and Evolution* summarizing the contributions of genetics up until that time toward our understanding of human history. They concluded the existing genetic and paleontological evidence points to a population "bottleneck" approximately two million years ago, stating, "We believe this bottleneck could have been the speciation event at the beginning of the lineage leading to living human populations."[91]

From a small population in the thousands, a new species emerged with theretofore unseen anatomical characteristics and behavioral traits. These included a dramatic increase in brain size, physical stature, hunting/gathering activities, and the use of tools. The scientists mentioned above observed, "These behavioral changes are far more massive and sudden than any earlier changes known for hominids," and concluded:

> *Our interpretation is that the changes are sudden and interrelated and reflect a bottleneck that was created because of the isolation of a small group...in other words, a genetic revolution.*[92]

Further genetic research brought this idea of a population bottleneck even further into the future of human development. Within the human cell, there is a form of DNA, called mitochondrial DNA (mtDNA), lying outside the cell nucleus that does not recombine during reproduction and thus accumulates evidence of hereditary changes that can be analyzed. The 2005 *Encyclopedia Britannica* cites genetic research using mtDNA suggesting *Homo sapiens* originated from a small population that existed about 150,000 years ago in Africa:

> *Homo sapiens is now crammed into virtually every habitable region of Earth, yet our species still bears the hallmarks of its origin as a tiny population inhabiting one small corner of the world. The variation in DNA among all the widespread human populations of today is less than what is found in any population of living apes. This is very surprising, given that there are so few apes in such small geographic areas...The inevitable conclusion is that ancestral H. sapiens quite recently passed through a "bottleneck" in which the entire human population was reduced to a few hundred or perhaps a couple of thousand individuals, perhaps approximately one hundred and fifty thousand years ago. Such a population size would be sufficiently small for a set of unique traits to become established...H. sapiens is not simply an incremental improvement on previous hominids...[but] is an entirely unprecedented phenomenon.*[93]

A more recent study of human genetic history was published by the Royal Society in 2009, confirming a population bottleneck in Africa and concluding, "There is a strong consensus that modern humans originated in Africa and moved out to colonize the world approximately fifty thousand years ago."[94]

I am not qualified to draw too many conclusions from this research on bottlenecks in human genetic history. Obviously whatever original population existed at the beginning of a bottleneck came from somewhere. Earlier hominids did exist, and modern genetics seems to support a common ancestry of humans with other earlier species even though those species became extinct.

Research has shown clearly, however, that humans were not just an "incremental improvement" in a long hominid line. They possessed very distinct anatomical features and quickly developed cognitive abilities, in sharp contrast to all predecessors. The ultimate example of this was the development of language, a capability not associated with any other species. Language gave humans the ability to communicate with each other, to accumulate knowledge, and to transfer knowledge to succeeding generations. A creature had emerged unlike any other in the hominid line or in the natural world, with the ability to manipulate its environment, and who, at some point in its long history, became conscious of itself.

> **Mind**, n. A mysterious form of matter secreted by the brain. Its chief activity consists in the endeavor to ascertain its own nature, the futility of the attempt being due to the fact that it has nothing but itself to know itself with.[95]

CHAPTER THIRTEEN

"You Are Nothing but a Pack of Neurons"

Most of us seldom think about thinking. There's a bumper sticker that kind of says it all: "Consciousness: that annoying time between naps."[96] The gray matter in our heads does its thing unnoticed, quietly regulating all our bodily functions and interactions with the world around us. Between the moment when I feel hungry and when I eat dinner, my brain is busy. It continues to regulate every breath and heartbeat. It generates a little explosion of neural signals and muscle contractions to get me to a standing position and walking toward the kitchen. It processes everything in my field of vision and guides me in the right direction through the house. It makes a preference known for what I want to eat more or less in accordance with my limited ability to prepare it. While the canned soup is heating, it brings thoughts about my wife, Lani, who is out of town, and a visualization of her having dinner. Somehow even a brief image of God looking down on us both comes to me, and a prayer forms in my mind for her safe return.

There is obviously a lot going on within the outwardly unimpressive lump of gray matter that we call the brain. Thanks to decades of progress in neuroscience, we now know quite a lot about this amazingly complex part of the human body and are learning more continuously about its structure and functions.

We know that the largest part of the brain is the cerebrum, which is divided into right and left cerebral hemispheres. The outer portion is the cerebral cortex, where computational activity occurs, while the inner portion consists of long nerve fibers carrying signals to and from other parts of the brain. The cerebellum, resembling two small balls, is located behind and below the cerebrum and is responsible for the largely unconscious coordination and control of the body's functions. Other smaller portions of the brain, such as the thalamus, hypothalamus, hippocampus, pons, and medulla, perform other highly specialized functions.

Each hemisphere of the cerebral cortex has four regions, classified as the frontal, parietal, temporal, and occipital lobes. Although these do not act independently of each other, they are associated generally with separate functions. The frontal lobes deal with initiative, planning, and general coordination of action; the parietal lobes with spatial perception and motor control; the temporal lobes with the integration of perceptual information we gain through speech and vision; and the occipital lobes with vision itself.

Another way to view the total range of brain activities is to consider its three main functional areas. The first, or primary, area is concerned with the maintenance and general regulation of the body, including the brain itself. The secondary area relates the individual to the external world by gathering and interpreting sensory information. The tertiary area converts perceptions into abstract thoughts, forms intentions and plans, and controls the actions of the individual.[97]

All this activity within the brain is performed at the cellular level by the body's nerve cells or neurons, of which about one hundred different types have been identified. Each has a soma or cell body containing a nucleus, dendrites that send incoming signals to the soma, and an elongated axon or nerve fiber that carries signals away from the soma. The axon has many branches and sub-branches that terminate in synaptic knobs. When a synaptic knob of one neuron attaches to a dendrite of another, a synapse is formed. A typical neuron can process signals at the rate of one thousand per second and can form synapses with from one thousand to ten thousand other neurons. Certain cells within the cerebellum are known to have eighty thousand synaptic knobs. In total the brain is composed of an estimated one hundred billion neurons[98] with more than one hundred trillion possible neural-network connections.[99] As a noted science writer recently put it, "The brain is the most complex structure in the known universe."[100]

Modern neuroscience continues to build on this knowledge of the brain and its components and to investigate the higher functions of human intelligence, such as reasoning, problem solving, learning, emotions, and language. The most basic question of all is that of consciousness. Somehow these billions of neural connections and myriad separate brain functions are not fragmented within the brain. They are integrated and unified into a single viewpoint. Somewhere within every person there is something that each of us thinks of as "me." By some amazing process, that "me" uses a physical neural network to produce abstract and ephemeral thoughts.

Historically and intuitively the idea has persisted that there is a mind separate from the brain that directs and uses the brain for its own purposes, and this mind accounts for human consciousness. Modern neuroscience now almost universally rejects this view. One text asserts, "The current school of thought regards mind as being a purely physical phenomenon" and quotes Carl Sagan: "My fundamental premise about the brain is that its workings—what we sometimes call 'mind'—are a consequence of anatomy and physiology and nothing else."[101] Nobel Laureate Francis Crick has stated:

> *You, your joys and sorrows, your memories and your ambitions, your sense of personal identity and free will are in fact no more than the behavior of a vast assembly of nerve cells and their associated molecules…You are nothing but a pack of neurons.*[102]

"YOU ARE NOTHING BUT A PACK OF NEURONS"

A philosophy professor asserts there is no satisfying answer to the question of what consciousness is, but that it results "when a rich hierarchy of neural systems transmits signals at a very high level of complexity," and since evolution is a given, we "know" that the "organization of neural complexity has been achieved by the accidental wisdom of natural selection."[103]

"Bad news, Dad—you're brain-dead!"

Mike Twohy[104]

I have great respect for these scientists and academicians who have devoted themselves to broadening our understanding of this complex field. However, we can see the pervasiveness of Darwinism in the assumptions underlying these views. I have found other expert testimony that gives a different perspective.

In *The Emperor's New Mind*, famous physicist and cosmologist Roger Penrose[105] analyzed the human thought process from the perspective of mathematics and computer design. Among many other issues, he addressed the possibility of constructing a computer to do what a human brain does. On this subject he observed:

> *Whereas unconscious actions of the brain are ones that proceed according to algorithmic processes, the action of consciousness is quite different, and it proceeds in a way that cannot be described by any algorithm.*[106]

In Penrose's view, judgment is required where rules haven't been laid out in advance, and judgments are the "manifestations of consciousness. We must 'see' the truth of a mathematical argument to be convinced of its validity. This 'seeing' is the very essence of consciousness."[107] He concluded:

> *In this book, I have presented many arguments intending to show the untenability of the viewpoint that our thinking is basically the same as the action of some very complicated computer. Is it not "obvious" that mere computation cannot evoke pleasure or pain; that it cannot perceive poetry or the beauty of an evening sky or the magic of sounds; that it cannot hope or love or despair; that it cannot have a genuine autonomous purpose? Yet science seems to have driven us to accept that we are all merely small parts of a world governed in full detail by very precise mathematical laws.*[108]

"YOU ARE NOTHING BUT A PACK OF NEURONS"

There is another interesting perspective on this subject from the field of medicine. Many consider Wilder Penfield the father of modern neurosurgery. Over a forty-year career of treating patients suffering from seizures, epilepsy, and other nervous-system disorders, he pioneered the mapping of the cerebral cortex and other areas of the brain. He performed many operations, of necessity, on conscious patients whose feedback he relied on during surgery. This enabled many successful operations as well as the accumulation of new and unique knowledge about the geography of the human brain.

His most startling realization, and the one he did not expect, was that within each patient there was always a "self" that stood apart from the actions of the brain. If he caused a patient to move his hand by applying an electrode to the relevant spot on the cerebral cortex, the patient would comment, "I didn't do that. You did." If he stimulated movement in one hand, often the patient would reach over to stop it with the other. He could cause movements of the head, eyes, and various limbs and even stimulate vivid recollections and flashbacks. Always, however, the patient remained aloof, passing judgment on everything that was happening. Penfield concluded this self-consciousness was an activity of the mind, distinct from other activity of the brain. None of his research could explain the phenomenon, and he was left with the belief that "The mind remains a mystery."[109]

Another mysterious manifestation of mental activity has been reported by people having "near-death experiences." These have been so widespread and subject to media attention in recent years that we are all familiar with stories of people who report leaving their bodies, going through a tunnel, seeing a bright light, etc. What we may not realize is this phenomenon has been the subject of extensive and systematic study. In 1976 Dr. Raymond Moody first reported more than one hundred case studies of people who had experienced clinical death and were subsequently revived. He found certain common experiences, including feelings of peacefulness, so-called out-of-body experiences, and travel into a heaven-like place.

Dr. Michael Sabom, a cardiologist, organized studies of near-death experiences during the 1980s and '90s that were even more objective.[110] He collected data from patients who had undergone near-death crisis events, such as cardiac arrest, coma, and life-threatening accidents, followed by some resuscitative procedures. He found that 43 percent reported some type of near-death experience. There was no correlation to age, sex, family background, or religious affiliation. Almost every person had the conscious feeling that he or she had experienced death, and the experience had taken place "outside their physical body."[111] There was a common emotional perception of peace and tranquility. To varying degrees many reported passing through a dark region and coming into light and a transcendent environment. A large majority of those who had this experience reported increased belief in an afterlife.

These experiences have obvious implications for our understanding of the mind. They all share a common feature in that they occurred outside the physical body. Some people reported them as true out-of-body experiences where the "self" separated from the physical body to observe events from outside or above. Some reported passages of their own consciousnesses into new regions or dimensions apart from the earthly surroundings of their physical bodies. In every case there was a part of the individual or an aspect of the individual's existence that was able to transcend the physical limits of the body and brain.

I conclude from this scientific and quasi-scientific information that there is simply a lot we do not know about human consciousness. Neuroscience has gone a long way toward explaining the neural processes of the brain but not very far toward a satisfactory explanation of why most ordinary people think there is more to being human than the operation of these neural processes alone.

Man has been defined as the "self-conscious" animal. This trait distinguishes him from all other living creatures. We have seen some of the scientific and philosophical speculation about the timing, cause, and mechanism for the origin of this distinctive characteristic. Even understanding what consciousness is has been a formidable challenge. The question remains: is consciousness a physical process of the brain and explainable through the evolutionary process, or did this unique feature of natural history come into existence by some other means?

If human consciousness were merely a physical activity of the human brain that had evolved through the process of natural selection, we would have another powerful argument against a role or need for God in the natural world. If there is a natural cause for everything, then everything that goes on within our minds must have a natural cause—even our spiritual lives.

I have found that the scientific evidence does not support this conclusion. Instead, I believe, we see again how some with scientists' perspectives go beyond their true expertise to make assertions that reflect their own faith in a materialistic belief system. These experts take conceptual leaps to fill in many blanks representing what is unknown and, to them, even mysterious about human consciousness.

From my perspective the concept of an autonomous mind separate from the physical brain seems pretty reasonable. My brain can do arithmetic when my mind decides it needs to. I know I can decide right now whether to get up from my chair or not. Science can find no physical or chemical cause that will determine my choice or predict it. My mind can turn its thoughts to cleaning out the closet or to contemplating the amazing nature of a limitless universe. It can conceive a poem, appreciate a painting, express love, and reflect on the spiritual possibilities of each. I lean toward Wilder Penrose's conclusion that the mind does truly remain an amazing and awe-inspiring mystery.

There is another explanation for human consciousness that we won't be able to confirm or deny through science. The Bible asserts, "God created man in his own image,"[112] and, "He has also set eternity in the hearts of men."[113] If true, this description of man's origin and nature would be a rather complete explanation for human consciousness and for all the spontaneous, creative, and transcendental dimensions of which it is capable.

> As an adolescent I aspired to lasting fame, I craved factual certainty, and I thirsted for a meaningful vision of human life—so I became a scientist. This is like becoming an archbishop so you can meet girls.
> —Matt Cartmill[114]

> There is something fascinating about science. One gets such wholesale returns of conjecture out of such a trifling investment of fact.
> —Mark Twain[115]

CHAPTER FOURTEEN

A Summary of the Science

It is clear that science has impacted practically every aspect of modern life, and, in every material sense, this has been to mankind's benefit. However, when it comes to considerations of purpose and meaning, many scientists and academicians are quietly cementing the impression that these subjects are irrelevant. I happen to believe that purpose and meaning are issues of ultimate importance. The fact that we ask such questions defines us as human beings. So, even as a nonexpert, I have undertaken my own mission to seek an understanding of how science is influencing my own and others' beliefs. If you are a scientist or an academician, I hope I have not offended you with my questions.

The most problematic area of science for religious believers has been evolutionary biology. Since I am not a biologist, I have tried to address this subject cautiously. I appreciate that this field has become one of the great organizing principles not only of biology but of much of modern science. Darwin's theories laid the foundation for the belief that natural, evolutionary processes can explain every complex feature of the world we know. This view has inevitably conflicted with religious belief and has historically been a flashpoint of conflict between science and religion.

Public battles have led to hardening of attitudes on both sides. Scientists recall the early church's persecutions of their forebears. They have seen creationists argue against scientific findings that conflict with literal interpretations of the Bible. They zealously guard against religious intrusions into science. Believers, on the other hand, see many scientists working from a materialistic belief system, unwilling to consider any evidence or even possibility of a higher intelligence or intentional design underlying the natural world.

Some religious people may still be trying to prove the literal interpretation of the Bible. At this point, however, most are simply trying to guard against a completely materialistic view of the world. The modern debate over what our children should hear in school is not, for the most part, a religious challenge to science. Most thoughtful religious people believe in science and don't seek to inject religion into science classes. However, there is great antipathy toward scientists who go beyond the findings of science itself or who rely on unproven assumptions to teach our children that life is governed only by the random processes of nature and therefore ultimately lacking in any transcendent meaning.

Skeptical readers may consider it naive on my part to offer an easy answer to this conflict. Nevertheless I am drawn to what many ordinary religious believers have all along felt intuitively about science and evolution. That is, this vast body of amazing scientific knowledge, including evolutionary biology, gives us insight into how a creator brought forth the natural world and oversees its progress. The more science reveals, the more we learn about the intricate, complex, and awe-inspiring nature of whatever created it.

"*Sometimes I wonder if there's more to life than unlocking the mysteries of the universe.*"

Bruce Eric Kaplan[116]

This outlook is based on one very large assumption: there are important aspects of the natural world that do not have demonstrable natural causes and for which science has no explanations. A corollary to this is the indisputable fact that there are important aspects of human existence that cannot be analyzed by the scientific method at all. In other words there is at least room to consider the existence of a divine hand in the universe.

So I return to the question we started with at the beginning. Has science explained the world around us to the extent that we can believe there is a natural cause for everything? Or is there room left for belief in an intelligent and purposeful design underlying what we see in the world? The previous chapters support the latter view in three instances.

A SUMMARY OF THE SCIENCE

First, the laws of physics so far seem to prove conclusively that the universe started with the Big Bang, and these laws account for every step in the subsequent creation of the elements and structures of the universe. However, physics is unable to explain the first event. Also, neither physics nor mathematical probability can explain the universal constants set into place at the moment of the Big Bang, which determines the very existence of the universe. So far a natural cause has not been found for the first cause.

Second, microbiology has discovered that the information-rich content of DNA governs amino-acid sequencing in the formation of proteins, cells, tissues, organs, and complete living organisms. Theories about the origin of DNA have been proposed, all based on the a priori assumptions of evolution and chemical necessity. The spontaneous self-assembly of amino acids and the origin of DNA still remain matters of pure speculation by biologists. There is certainly room to question the existence of any natural cause or process leading to the origin of life.

Finally, we come to human beings. In considering the long process of our development, we see a different pattern from the rest of the animal kingdom. The species *Homo sapiens* seems to have originated at some time in the past with very distinct anatomical and cognitive features. This species went on to inhabit every corner of the globe, experiencing an explosion in mental, social, cultural, scientific, and spiritual development unlike anything else in the natural world.

Along the way this species became conscious of the world and of itself. Even though most scientists believe this consciousness developed naturally, they don't know how. No one knows whether increased brain size led to this unique activity or whether the brain grew *because* of it. There is ample room for the scientist and nonscientist alike to conclude that no natural cause is likely to be proven for human consciousness and that this phenomenon remains a true mystery that science cannot explain. There is something that constitutes the self other than the physical brain. This something is capable of autonomous thought and action and is able to contemplate eternity and its own place in it. It seems easy for many to believe that intelligence evolved from matter. Why should it be so difficult to believe that intelligence came first?

In reaching these conclusions, we don't have to challenge evolution or science. Furthermore, any believer who agrees with my conclusions must be prepared to accept certain parts of the Bible as representing general truth, not historical or scientific fact. In fact most believers I have met seem to perceive no conflict between God's word in scripture and the great body of scientific knowledge available to us today.

On this subject, a book recently written by Francis S. Collins, the nation's leading geneticist and longtime director of the Human Genome Project, has informed and inspired me. After a lifetime devoted to science and genetic research, he has argued forcefully for a truce between science and religion. He proposes the following premises to support a synthesis of religious and scientific belief:

1. *The universe came into being out of nothingness approximately fourteen billion years ago.*

2. *Despite massive improbabilities, the properties of the universe appear to have been precisely tuned for life.*

3. *While the precise mechanism of the origin of life on Earth remains unknown, once life arose, the processes of evolution and natural selection permitted the development of biological diversity and complexity over long periods of time.*

4. *Once evolution got underway, no special supernatural intervention was required.*

A SUMMARY OF THE SCIENCE

5. Humans are part of this process, sharing a common ancestor with the great apes.

6. But humans are also unique in ways that defy evolutionary explanation and point to our spiritual nature.[117]

According to Collins these simple statements show the way for both sides to an "intellectually satisfying and logically consistent" synthesis of world views. There need be no contradictions between the findings of science and the beliefs of the great monotheistic religions of the world.

At this point I need to make a further observation about the textbooks and scientific references I have consulted on these subjects. Countless volumes inform us about the findings of science, presenting every detail by means of exhaustive explanations, charts, diagrams, and photographs. They present the facts thoroughly and precisely. For instance, in neuroscience texts, I have read about the variety of neurons and their submicroscopic components, how each functions, how they all interrelate to the whole. I discovered a new and intricate world dealing with the inner functioning of the brain.

What is missing from these texts and from most other biology texts, however, is any sense of amazement or even wonder at these facts. Such an attitude may be unscientific, but it seems a shame to leave students with an understanding of the details of neurobiology but no commensurate sense of awe about this knowledge.

I think there is a lot to be said for a genuine wonder about the natural world and universe, including those areas understood in scientific terms and those we do not understand. Even the unreligious physicist Paul Davies has exclaimed, "I rejoice in the lawfulness of the universe and in the beautiful nature of the laws of physics."[118] The natural universe is amazingly ordered, complex, beautiful, and, to the extent that it is unknown, mysterious.

We will never know all the universe's mysteries. But even if someday all of the blanks were filled in by science, we would still be left with the question, *Why* has it happened? Even if we knew how the universe began and what preceded it, what the process was for the origin of life, and what determines human consciousness, we would still not grasp a reason or a purpose for it. As Richard Feynman stated when considering the confusion of the modern world, "The great accumulation of understanding…has a kind of meaninglessness about it."[119] Science that rules out the possibility of an organizing intelligence rules out the possibility of a purpose for the universe and for life itself, rendering everything ultimately meaningless.

I know that so far I have indulged in a lot of finger pointing at scientists and academicians and done little to prove God's existence. They could turn the question on me at this point and ask, Why does it have to be so difficult? Why isn't God obvious to us all? I have asked myself these questions many times, and I will share my thoughts on them in chapter twenty. But for now I hope my skeptical reader has some appreciation for how I came to the conclusion that science does not present an intellectual barrier to belief in God and even that his existence explains a lot that cannot be explained otherwise. There are, of course, many to whom God is indeed *very* obvious. Speaking from human intuition alone, and with reference to no scientific data, the biblical king David exclaimed, "The heavens declare the glory of God; the skies proclaim the work of his hands."[120]

> **Self-Evident**, adj. Evident to one's self and to nobody else.[121]

> For every expert, there is an equal and opposite expert.
> —Anonymous[122]

> To doubt everything or to believe everything are two equally convenient solutions; both dispense with the necessity of reflection.
> —Henri Poincare[123]

CHAPTER FIFTEEN
Is There Proof God Exists?

I don't think it controversial to state there are and have been vast numbers of human beings firmly convinced of God's existence. Most people probably come to this belief through childhood influences or associations with other believers. There are also some who have experienced more-direct insights and revelations through events in their lives. Then there are those who have undertaken the task of proving for themselves that God exists. In my case I cannot totally discount childhood experiences, although some of them were more negative than positive. I definitely had no revelations. What I now believe about God, I have proven, at least to myself.

Many others who are more qualified than I have undertaken this task. Great thinkers of the past have advanced the so-called "classical proofs." Anselm of Canterbury (c. AD 1033–1109) proposed the ontological argument that God can be demonstrated by intuition and reason alone. Anselm argued that God is the greatest entity that can be conceived. This conception of God obviously exists in human understanding. It would be a logical fallacy to say God does not also exist in reality since this would not be the greatest entity that can be conceived. Needless to say, this was a controversial assertion then and has had a long history of detractors since.

Thomas Aquinas (c. AD 1225–1274) adapted Aristotle's approach in proposing the first cosmological argument for God. He argued that every finite being has a cause, yet no finite being can cause itself. The causal chain has to originate somewhere. He considered God the first cause. This argument resonates more clearly in the modern age of cosmological consensus about the Big Bang origin of the universe.

Thomas Aquinas also proposed a proof of God we now know as the teleological or design argument. This was based on the perceived evidence of order and design in the processes of nature. Centuries of scientific progress have explained many aspects of this perceived order in purely natural terms. I have already described some very important areas where this does not seem to be the case and where there is a lot of room for belief in such a designer.

Unfortunately, I'm afraid, few skeptics, me included, have been or will be convinced of God's existence by logical proofs such as these. So far I may have somewhat dispelled the idea that science or logic have disproved God, and I may even have shown that the existence of God is often a better explanation for what we see in nature than anything science has suggested. As for specific proof of God, however, I will have to rely on my own logic to explain the basis of my belief, which constitutes my proof.

The origin and continued existence of the universe and the origin and evolution of life on Earth are strong indicators of an intelligent and all-powerful creator. The proof of such a creator is found in the nature of the most-amazing phenomenon that exists in the universe. This is clearly the individual human being, endowed with the mysterious and unfathomable trait of human consciousness. Somehow, from the organic matter that constitutes the human brain, transcendent thoughts of love, eternity, and God stream forth. All these thoughts are miraculously integrated into a single viewpoint within each person, constituting what we know as the self. Billions of these discrete entities constitute the human race. Despite centuries of dedicated effort by science, the essence of any individual human being has not been found in the complex biological components of the brain or the human body. The most logical source of such a complex and universal phenomenon is an intelligent and all-powerful creator.

Another aspect of the self is the ability to distinguish right and wrong, often referred to as the conscience. With few exceptions people in all cultures and geographic areas hold certain values and follow guides for behavior. Even though these values are not identical, they consistently include respect for the sanctity of life, honesty, and fairness in dealing with others. Acts of love and kindness are almost universally admired and treasured. Acts of true altruism and selflessness also occur, and they especially have no evolutionary explanation or benefit. The best explanation for human morality seems to be a truly wise and loving God who created humans in his own image. We humans embody God's image in our intelligence, capacity for love, longing to do right, and need for God himself.

Unfortunately we are pretty pale images of that creator and far from perfect. For his own reasons, God also inexplicably gave us the freedom of will to make choices and decisions. We are therefore able to make mistakes, act selfishly, and perform acts that are detrimental to others. So we have rarely achieved perfection in the exercise of our moral nature. I will discuss this "problem" and its solution in more detail later.

When I consider my proof of God's existence, I can't forget my resistance to such arguments for most of my life. True skepticism does not yield easily, if ever, to persuasion. Every argument has a counterargument, and no matter how hard we search, there is always more information that will shed new light on what we think we know.

An important aspect of the change in my skeptical attitude was a sense of wonder about the natural world. Whether considering the ordered complexity of the universe or the amazing nature of human love, I have sensed a miraculous aspect beyond the bounds of science or reason. Seeing the world from this point of view is undoubtedly a difficult leap for a skeptical person. It was an unexpected and surprising change in perspective for me. That this idea became an important part of my thought process is difficult to explain, although I will try in more detail later. For now I can only state I have looked at the evidence both analytically and with a sense of sincere wonder and have proven God's existence entirely to my satisfaction. The more I learn about science, nature, and the human condition, the more certain I am that I have reached the proper conclusion.

PART THREE

What about the Bible?

> **Mythology**, n. The body of a primitive people's beliefs concerning its origin, early history, heretics, deities and so forth, as distinguished from the true accounts, which it invents later.[124]

CHAPTER SIXTEEN

How Good Is the Good Book?

As a young boy working in the tobacco market in Conway, South Carolina, I had some interesting discussions with other workers and farmers around the backdoor of the warehouse late in the day, after the work was done. One of the usual characters in this scene was a man called "Preacher." No one seemed to know or question the official nature of his title. Preacher often took the conversation on a philosophical turn. One day he asserted, "Boys, I need to let you know that the Earth is square." After a few jeers and snickers, he went on to say, "It says in the Bible, 'I saw four angels standing at the four corners of the Earth.' And if it says in the Bible that the Earth has four corners, then it has to be square!"[125] Who could argue with such logic?

The Bible has been cited as "proof" of many things, some not as trivial as the shape of the Earth. In the nineteenth century, Southern ministers found support for slavery in the apostle Paul's words to the Ephesians: "Slaves, obey your earthly masters with respect and fear."[126] Based on this and other verses mentioning slaves, a sizeable segment of the Southern theological establishment lined up solidly behind the righteousness of slavery as an institution. Early in life I found it difficult to take most of scripture seriously knowing that passages are picked out in this way to support particular viewpoints.

Over the centuries believers and unbelievers alike have used and abused the Bible for a multitude of purposes. It has been studied as history and read as literature. It has provided comfort and solace to those in need and has been used as a guide to living and source of inspiration for millions. Some have accepted it as true in a general sense while there have been, and still are, those who take it literally, word for word. There are probably many more today who consider it pure mythology.

"The Bible... that would be under self-help."

Peter Steiner[127]

Regardless of perspective, we cannot ignore the historical importance of this great book. The *Biblia Latina* was the first book reproduced on Gutenberg's printing press in 1454. Since then *billions* more have been published and distributed all over the world in practically every known language. As recently as 1998, the United Bible Societies dispensed more than forty million Bibles and testaments worldwide.[128] No book in history comes close to this level of continuing circulation.

The Bible's vast readership, multilayered themes, and spiritual depth have made it a major determinant of Western civilization. It has been the sourcebook of the world's most widespread religion. It has provided symbols, characters, plots, and inspiration to generations of artists, writers, and musicians. Its themes are interwoven into the legal, social, and political systems of liberal democratic governments. The United States of America was founded specifically on the biblical view of man as a being created in God's image. The dignity and rights of individual citizens were therefore based on the authority of the Bible and God, not rulers or governments.

Christians believe that the Bible is in essence the story of God's plan for mankind—why human beings were created, how they are wonderful but imperfect, why they are unable to make themselves perfect, and the simple way God intends for them to find him in this life and in eternity. These truths are simple in themselves, but they are revealed in the complex events collected in this wide-ranging volume. More than forty writers working independently over a thousand years to produce sixty-six separate books (as counted by Protestant Christians) accomplished this feat. The first thirty-nine represent the total of Hebrew scripture, referred to as the *Tanakh* by Jews and as the Old Testament by Christians. The remaining twenty-seven books comprise the New Testament.

> **History**, n. The race between education and catastrophe.[129]

> Say what you will about the Ten Commandments, you must always come back to the pleasant fact that there are only ten of them.
> —H. L. Mencken[130]

CHAPTER SEVENTEEN

A New Look at the Old Testament

The Old Testament is, in essence, the story of God's revealing himself to an obscure tribe of Semitic nomads during a turbulent and formative period in ancient history. The action spans the area known historically as the Fertile Crescent, extending in an arc from ancient Egypt along the Mediterranean coast through Mesopotamia to the Persian Gulf. At around 2,000 BC, the area known in modern times as Palestine lay along the narrow strip of land between the Mediterranean Sea and the Arabian Desert, at the focal point of the trade and invasion routes between Egypt and Mesopotamia. By then these two regions, one at either end of the crescent, had produced well-established civilizations with cultures far in advance of any other area of the Western world. Of particular importance, they had developed written languages for storytelling, record keeping, and commerce.

From a modern perspective, this may seem an obscure setting for God to reveal himself and his expectations for mankind. However, many consider this time and place the true dawn of civilization. From geographical and historical perspectives, it would have been a very strategic time and place to plant and germinate an important seed.

"We're slugs—we don't have a creation myth."

Charles Barsotti[131]

Overview

The Old Testament covers a lot of territory in time, geography, and subject matter. The first five books are referred to variously as the Pentateuch, the Torah, or the law and include Genesis, Exodus, Leviticus, Numbers, and Deuteronomy. Following the stories of the creation and the great flood, Abraham appeared as the early central figure. This first of the great patriarchs responded to God's call, journeying with his family out of Mesopotamia and into Palestine to become the founding father of the great monotheistic religions: Judaism, Islam, and Christianity. Abraham's covenant with God was passed through succeeding generations that eventually became the tribes of Israel. The history of these people is chronicled through their captivity in Egypt, escape under Moses, and forty years wandering in the desert. During this time God revealed many facets of his character and laws and, through great trials, gradually molded these tribes into a nation.

Twelve other historical books follow the Torah. In Joshua we learn how the Israelites began their conquest and settlement of Canaan, the promised land, at a time estimated around 1,200 BC.[132] The book of Judges describes years of continued warfare under dynamic but flawed leaders, such as Gideon and Samson. The two books of Samuel chronicle the establishment of a monarchy and the reign of the famous King David. In the first book of Kings, we learn how David's son, Solomon, brought peace and prosperity during a time remembered by Jews as their Golden Age. Unfortunately Solomon's flaws eventually led to chaos and a split kingdom—Israel in the north and Judah in the south. The second book of Kings describes the Assyrian Empire's conquest of Israel and Judah, Nebuchadnezzar's destruction of Jerusalem in 597 BC, and the exile of the Jews to Babylon.[133] Ezra and Nehemiah tell the story of their eventual return under the Persian king Cyrus and the rebuilding of the Jerusalem temple and city walls by 444 BC.[134]

This history of Israel was followed by a series of literary works, or sacred writings, including the book of Job, Psalms, Proverbs, Ecclesiastes, and Song of Songs. Job presents the difficult story of a good man's suffering through misfortune. After hearing all the worldly explanations and rationalizations, he finally challenged God about his plight and received the final answer in God's greatest tirade:

> *Who is this that darkens my counsel with words without knowledge? Brace yourself like a man; I will question you, and you shall answer me. Where were you when I laid the earth's foundation? Tell me, if you understand. Who marked off its dimensions?*[135]

The other literary books are poetic in nature and have provided comfort, inspiration, and wisdom to religious and nonreligious readers over the centuries. Nowhere else can we discover such eloquent insights:

He has also set eternity in the hearts of men.[136]

The fear of the Lord is the beginning of knowledge.[137]

Though it cost all you have, get understanding.[138]

The path of the righteous is like the first gleam of dawn.[139]

Pride goes before destruction, a haughty spirit before a fall.[140]

As no one is discharged in time of war, so wickedness will not release those who practice it.[141]

The remaining seventeen books of the Old Testament contain the writings of the Hebrew prophets. Isaiah, Jeremiah, Ezekiel, and Daniel are considered the major prophets due primarily to the length of their works. Many of the prophets focused on Israel and Judah's precarious condition under the threat of an expansive Assyrian Empire and on the poor moral condition of their own people. Isaiah, Jeremiah, and others foretold the destruction to come. The prophets generally framed national events present, past, and future in relation to God's expectations and called repeatedly for a return to faithfulness. A recurring theme was the prediction of a future redeemer or Messiah who would save Israel and the world. Isaiah repeatedly foretold God's ultimate purpose for Israel: "I will also make you a light for the Gentiles, that you may bring my salvation to the ends of the earth."[142]

In these prophecies Christians find a link between the Old and New Testaments, as Jesus Christ is apparently described and foretold centuries before his appearance in the world. Isaiah described a "Prince of Peace" and suffering servant who "carried our sorrows," "was pierced for our transgressions," and would eventually heal the world "by his wounds."[143] Zechariah described a king who will be "gentle and riding on a donkey" and "the one they have pierced."[144]

Jeremiah foretold a new relationship to come between God and his people that would go beyond conformity to the written law of the Old Testament: "I will put my law in their minds and write it on their hearts. I will be their God, and they will be my people."[145] In this new paradigm, transformation from the inside would become more important than outward appearances.

History of the Old Testament

The story of how this scripture has come down to us today is complex and, in its early stages, uncertain. The stories of the creation, the patriarchs, and early Israel were transmitted orally for generations. The learning and faithful transmissions of histories by word of mouth was a common feature of many early cultures. The epic Greek poems attributed to Homer were passed down orally for centuries before being written down.[146]

Aside from the Ten Commandments written on tablets by God himself, the first biblical mention of written scripture comes with the Lord's command to Moses: "Set up some large stones and coat them with plaster. Write on them all the words of this law."[147] During the reign of King David, in about 1000 BC, the importance of the written word was apparent in the hierarchy of the royal court: "Joab son of Zeruiah was over the army; Jehoshaphat son of Ahilud was recorder."[148] Scribes are mentioned prominently thereafter throughout the Old Testament, giving a clear indication of the importance attached to the accurate recording of events.

During the reign of King Josiah in about 620 BC, there is a story referring specifically to written scripture:

A NEW LOOK AT THE OLD TESTAMENT

> *Then Shaphan the secretary informed the king, "Hilkiah the priest has given me a book." And Shaphan read from it in the presence of the king. When the king heard the words of the Book of the Law, he tore his robes.*[149]

The oldest surviving Old Testament documents written in Hebrew were discovered in 1947 by a Bedouin shepherd who discovered a cave in the Wadi Qumran, near the north coast of the Dead Sea. Over the next ten years, archaeologists combed the area, resulting in the collection of more than one hundred biblical manuscripts written in Hebrew on papyrus and leather scrolls. The Dead Sea Scrolls were found to contain portions of every Old Testament book except Esther, including a twenty-three-foot scroll containing the complete book of Isaiah.[150] All sixty-six chapters were included and were largely in agreement with modern texts. These documents have been radiocarbon dated back to the second and third centuries BC[151] The scrolls are a testament to the diligence of the Jewish scribes who worked under the strictest regulation over many centuries to preserve and pass down their sacred texts.

The earliest translation of the Hebrew Old Testament into Greek occurred in about 250 BC thanks to the Jewish population then living in Egypt, who needed scripture in the language native to their culture.[152] The actual work is attributed to seventy-two Jewish scribes from Israel, each working in isolation to produce a single perfect translation. Although the authenticity of this story is uncertain, the name given the Greek version of the Old Testament has survived—*Septuagint*, which means "the seventy." This translation made the Hebrew scripture, which had been known until then only in the Jewish sanctuaries, available to the rest of the world through the most widely used language of the age. Eventually this Greek translation would be the scripture most used by early Christians.

The Greek Septuagint and Dead Sea Scrolls confirm the existence of a generally accepted body of Hebrew scriptures before the second century BC. The earliest recorded discussions to authorize certain books did not occur until AD 90–100, during an assembly of rabbis at the Jewish cultural center of Jamnia in central Israel. This council did not represent all Jews, and in fact no formal Jewish ecclesiastical authority ever ruled on the canonicity of Hebrew scriptures. Nevertheless, by the end of the first century AD, the books of the Tanakh, or Old Testament, had achieved almost universal acceptance within Judaism and Christianity.[153]

Archaeology

Archaeological discoveries have substantiated much of the history depicted in the Old Testament. There was a great upsurge in Middle Eastern exploration starting in the 1800s by scientists from Germany, France, England, and America. For more than two hundred years, archaeologists have dedicated themselves to searching for evidence to confirm or to question biblical places and events. Even though archeology is in many ways an inexact science, there are many very specific confirmations.

From 1933 to 1938, a French expedition discovered more than twenty thousand cuneiform tablets at the site of the ancient city of Mari, near present-day Abu Kemal on the Iraqi-Syrian border. Dated from 2000 to 1800 BC, these tablets mention many names found in the biblical accounts of the patriarchs, including Nahor and Haran.[154] These towns were confirmed as well-established cities during this era and were thus lifted out of a mythological context and placed solidly into history. The tablets also confirmed a flourishing trade and the existence of trade routes between Mesopotamia and the land of Canaan (later Palestine), making the travels of Abraham more plausible and less aimless than ever before thought.[155]

The first independent and contemporaneous documentation of the existence of Israel was found on an Egyptian monument from a mortuary temple near Thebes dated to about 1229 BC. The Cairo Museum now holds the monument, which describes the victorious campaigns of the Pharaoh Merenptah, including the inscription: "Canaan is despoiled and all its evil with it. The people of Israel is desolate, it has no offspring: Palestine has become a widow for Egypt."[156]

Thanks to the discovery of numerous monuments and libraries from the Assyrian and Babylonian Empires, large sections of the Bible have been confirmed from 924 to 597 BC. The Harper *Atlas of the Bible* presents a table with translations from these sources compared to specific biblical verses and concludes:

> *The overlapping of Assyrian and biblical accounts of various events makes possible an absolute chronology for the kingdoms of Israel and Judah. Assyrian kings kept records of the years of their reigns...from the beginnings of the ninth through to the end of the sixth century BC... [the] absolute date for a certain year in the reign of an Assyrian king makes possible the assignment of dates to the biblical kings whose history was interwoven with that of the kings of Assyria.*[157]

Summary

Much of the Old Testament is clearly based on real people and actual events. Even so, I should point out there are degrees to which we should take some passages literally. The creation story is a good example. Some Christians consider every detail in Genesis to be factual as presented, down to the length of each day as twenty-four actual hours. Others consider this biblical account to be more representational of *what* God did than of *how* he did it. Regardless of how these details are interpreted, all seem to agree on the great underlying truths being presented: that God created the world and all that is in it and created mankind in his image.

The fact that much of the Old Testament has been proven factual does not prove that it was divinely inspired. However, the fact that it has been proven to be so much more than mythology is important. The realization that so many places and events were real gives us great assurance that in most cases, we are reading actual history. The care with which this information has been passed down through the ages gives great confidence in its consistency and accuracy.

A distinctive feature of these narratives and of much of the rest of the Bible is the humanity of the characters. We see all their strengths and weaknesses. Abraham was obedient to God but also stood up to God to argue for the "good" people of Sodom. Moses was a great leader but frequently subject to doubt, frustration, and anger. The great kings, David and Solomon, had their tragic weaknesses. The flaws and failures of these biblical figures are never glossed over. As these imperfect heroes struggle in their humanness, we sense an element of truth lacking in mythology. We also get glimpses of a demanding and, at times, stern God but also a God who shows mercy and patience with those who faithfully seek him.

It is amazing that all this information was meticulously preserved for a single purpose—to reveal God's nature and expectations for humanity. It was clearly not written to glorify the Israelites or any of their leaders, as every flaw and failure seems to have been faithfully recorded. In fact we finally are left with the clear picture that no human being has the integrity and will to consistently live up to the righteousness of God.

Very few great ancient or modern historical works were produced for such a purpose. When considering the depth and complexity of the Old Testament's imagery and themes, I have felt compelled to at least ask the question, Could human writers have just dreamed up all this? Or could this be how God truly began to reveal himself to mankind? Somehow these stories and their imperfect characters continue to convey a higher spiritual truth that absorbs and inspires millions.

> **Christian**, n. One who believes that the New Testament is a divinely inspired book admirably suited to the spiritual needs of his neighbor.[158]

CHAPTER EIGHTEEN

And Then Came the New Testament

There are few people in the world who do not know *something* about Jesus Christ. Since our calendars are dated from his birth, we know he lived two thousand years ago. We also know he lived in the same geographical setting described in the preceding chapter. His life and ministry were brief. He relied on a small group of ordinary men to assist him in his ministry and to learn his message. We know that this message lived on after him, transforming men and women in widening circles to become the basis of the world's most widespread religion. No other single person, political figure, military leader, or philosopher has impacted the world to such an extent. The New Testament is his story.

Much was written about Jesus during the first century, after his death. These letters and stories circulated among Jesus's followers and between the early churches. The texts were considered authentic and based on the earliest observations of his life and ministry and gradually became accepted as scripture and were eventually selected for inclusion in a New Testament. This new body of scripture came to include twenty-seven books written by as many as eleven authors, with an overall length about one third of the Old Testament. The historical period covered was from about 5 BC to AD 70, including thirty-three years of Jesus's life[159] and approximately thirty-five years of the growth of the early church. It should be understood that most of this material was written and preserved as both a statement of faith and a historical account.

Overview

The heart of the New Testament and basis of Christianity are found in the four Gospels:[160] Matthew, Mark, Luke, and John. These books present similar but different versions of the life, death, and teachings of Jesus, and his words are featured prominently in each. Traditionally Matthew and John are thought to have been apostles of Christ whereas Mark and Luke were companions to the apostles, once removed from the true source. These authors are not mentioned directly in their respective texts although their identities seem to have been firmly established very early in church tradition. These writers, their sources, and the exact dates of their writings have been the subjects of scholarly investigation and debate for centuries.

The book of Matthew ties the New Testament directly to the Old Testament and seems to have been written mainly for the benefit of the Jewish community. It includes a genealogy of Jesus, establishing his line of descent from Abraham. There are more than forty direct citations of Old Testament scriptures to establish the case that Jesus is the fulfillment of those scriptures. When interrogated by Jewish officials as to his opinion about the greatest commandment, Jesus put more than twenty chapters of Old Testament rules and regulation into a new perspective with his reply:

> *Love the Lord your God with all your heart and with all your soul and with all your mind. This is the first and greatest commandment. And the second is like it: Love your neighbor as yourself. All the Law and the Prophets hang on these two commandments.*[161]

He made it even simpler with his statement which we now know as the Golden Rule: "So in everything, do to others what you would have them do to you."[162] He consistently de-emphasized ritual for its own sake and religious practice for its outward appearance, saying to his critics, "I desire mercy, not sacrifice."[163]

The highlight of Matthew is Jesus's Sermon on the Mount, presented in three chapters, containing some of the most startling ethical teachings of all time:

> *You have heard that it was said… "Do not murder…" But I tell you that anyone who is angry with his brother will be subject to judgment. You have heard that it was said, "Love your neighbor and hate your enemy." But I tell you: Love your enemies and pray for those who persecute you. Be careful not to do your "acts of righteousness" before men, to be seen by them. Blessed are the poor in spirit…the meek…the merciful…the pure in heart…the peacemakers.*[164]
>
> *Whoever wants to become great among you must be your servant.*[165]
>
> *Unless you change and become like little children, you will never enter the kingdom of heaven.*[166]

These teachings amazed his audiences but did not endear Jesus to the religious establishment of the time or fulfill the prevailing hope for a conquering Messiah who would lead Israel to a new day of power and independence.

The Gospels of Mark and Luke are similar to Matthew's and share many similar passages. Scholars believe that much of the material for these books came from a common source. Each book relates the story of the transfiguration in which God appeared to Jesus and several disciples while together on a mountaintop. Jesus was surrounded by a dazzling aura as God proclaimed, "This is my Son, whom I love."[167] In these books Jesus declared unequivocally that he was God's son and that "All authority in heaven and on Earth has been given to me."[168] All the Gospels present the story of his death at the hands of Jewish and Roman authorities, each with different details. Each Gospel then describes the most important events of the entire Bible: Jesus's resurrection from the dead, his appearances to others, and his ascension into heaven.

The Gospel of John is unique in its theological emphasis and is even more explicit in establishing Jesus's divinity. This book opens with a declaration that Jesus was with God in the beginning, was God himself, and that he "became flesh and made his dwelling among us."[169] Again, making the connection to the Old Testament, John asserts, "For the law was given through Moses: grace and truth came through Jesus Christ."[170] John quotes Jesus as he revealed the central theme of his ministry (also the basis of Christianity and the most widely known and memorized verse in the Bible): "For God so loved the world that he gave his one and only Son, that whoever believes in him shall not perish but have eternal life."[171] Throughout this book Jesus eloquently asserts his divine nature as "the bread of life," "the light of the world," "the good shepherd," and "the way, the truth, and the life." There is no room to misinterpret who he and his followers thought he was. He also made it clear that his purpose was not to establish a new system of civic or religious authority in Israel or anywhere else, stating, "My kingdom is not of this world."[172]

The Book of Acts serves as a historical bridge between the Gospels and the rest of the New Testament. After Jesus's departure his disciples were left to seek and organize followers and decide many key issues, such as the relationship between Jews and Gentiles in the new faith. Peter was a key figure; Jesus told him, "You are Peter, and on this rock I will build my church."[173] Another key figure was Saul of Tarsus, a Pharisee, who at first was a vigorous antagonist of Jesus's followers. However, after a miraculous conversion on the road to Damascus, Paul became the most ardent apostle of all. His missionary journeys to Asia Minor, Greece, and Rome and his letters to the young churches that he established are the subjects of much of the rest of the New Testament. These letters, or Epistles, provide additional history but mostly outline the formation of early Christian church doctrine.

History of the New Testament

These books of the New Testament were written in Greek during the first and second centuries. Although signed and dated copies have not survived, thousands of papyrus fragments with segments of these books have been found dating to the second and third centuries. The oldest is a piece of the Book of John dated to circa AD 125. According to Peter van Minnen, an expert in ancient documents, "The earliest papyrus manuscripts come very close to the time when the New Testament was written."[174]

During the second century, several early Christian writers confirmed the existence of a body of accepted writings about Jesus. The oldest list of New Testament books is found in a document called the Muratorian fragment, dated to AD 170 and found in 1740 by Ludovico Muratori in a library in Milan. This manuscript refers to the four Gospels, Acts, letters of Paul, and other letters being used within the church at that time.[175] Irenaeus, the head of the early church of Lyons in Gaul, wrote *Against Heresies* around AD 182–188 and referred to the Fourfold Gospel, citing each by name.[176]

The process of selecting and weeding out early writings to form the official canon of the New Testament went on until the early fifth century. In his *Epistola Festalis* (AD 367), Athanasius of Alexandria provided the first complete list of books included in the present Bible.[177] A Synod in Rome adopted Athanasius's list in 382, and Pope Gelasius ratified it in the next century. The oldest complete manuscript in existence is the *Codex Vaticanus*, dated to about AD 325; the Vatican has held it since the Middle Ages. One of the earliest complete manuscripts was found in 1859 by a German scientist exploring St. Catherine's Monastery near Mt. Sinai. The *Codex Sinaiticus*, dated to AD 350, is now part of the British Museum's holdings.

The life of Jesus and certain events of the New Testament are also confirmed by other contemporary, non-Christian sources. Jesus and Christians are mentioned in the writings of various Roman, Greek, and Jewish writers of the first and second centuries, such as Suetonious, Pliny the Younger, and Lucian of Samosata. Roman historian Tacitus wrote in AD 109 about the great fire in Rome and Emperor Nero's effort to shift the blame to a group called Christians:

> *Nero fastened the guilt and inflicted the most exquisite tortures on a class hated for their abominations, called Christians by the populace. Christus, from whom the name had its origin, suffered the extreme penalty during the reign of Tiberius at the hands of one of our procurators, Pontius Pilate.*[178]

The Jewish historian, Josephus, wrote about Jesus in the early 90s AD.

> *Now there was about this time Jesus, a wise man,* <u>*if it be lawful to call him a man*</u>*, for he was a doer of wonderful works,* <u>*a teacher of such men as receive the truth with pleasure.*</u> *He drew many over to him both of the Jews and the Gentiles.* <u>*He was the Christ;*</u> *and when Pilate, at the suggestion of the principal men among us, had condemned him to the cross, those that loved him at the first did not forsake him…and the tribe of Christians, so named from him, are not extinct to this day.*[179]

Josephus originally wrote in Greek, and all existing copies of his work contain this quote. However, the parts underlined are the subject of some controversy among historians, as some suspect that transcribers may have inserted them later or that some qualifying phrase such as "his followers believed" may have been lost. The rest of the quote compares to an Arabic version of Josephus's work from the fourth century, and most scholars accept it as authentic.[180]

These independent historians have documented the fact that a man named Jesus lived and preached early in the first century in the land known as Palestine, then under Roman rule, and he was put to death on a cross. A mass of detailed information about his ministry also comes from either first- or second-generation sources close to him. These early writers and followers considered Jesus the Son of God and long-awaited Jewish Messiah. The stories about Jesus include, in addition to his great ethical teachings, accounts of a virgin birth, healings, miracles, and Jesus's resurrection from the dead. There is no way to prove or disprove the historical truth of these assertions regarding his divinity. We are left only to wonder at the amazing transformation of those who knew him and of countless others whose lives have been changed when they've accepted these assertions as true.

The history of these early Christian writings has included controversies. For centuries scholars have analyzed the writings that were included in the canon. They have sought to prove or disprove the authorship of the various books and to identify the true source materials. Over the years many writings that were not included in the canon have come to light. These have also been analyzed thoroughly. Many New Testament critics contend that the accepted scriptures were selected or shaped to support a developing belief system rather than to report actual events. Others contend the teachings and personality of Jesus have been distorted to fit various agendas.

Theological inquiry of this nature continues today by serious scholars with both religious and secular interests. For example, a Gospel of Judas, dated to AD 220–340, has been recently publicized portraying the apostle, Judas Iscariot, in a different light from that of the traditional

Gospels. Occasionally, less serious efforts surface in popular culture, with books such as *The DaVinci Code* purporting to reveal conspiracy theories about the early church.

"Sure, the New Testament looks like a winner, but has it got legs?"

Lee Lorenz[181]

The history of the church and its sacred writings is obviously a fertile field for scholarly and less-than-scholarly examination. Analysis and interpretation of the Bible have been extensive endeavors producing a vast body of literature. Serious scholars and others have devoted their lives and careers to these subjects over the centuries, and libraries are filled with the results. There is a natural curiosity about all this material and its implications for the faith of believers.

In spite of this complex history, however, I have found much that remains certain about New Testament scripture. There is a clear historical record of extensive effort on the part of early Christians to identify the authentic works of those who knew Jesus or who were directly associated with his disciples. A core body of writings emerged very early that was widely accepted and circulated within the Christian community. The provenance of these writings has been scrupulously maintained since the second century. The volume of fragments and manuscripts confirming these writings and their proximity in date to actual events exceeds that of any other historical event of the ancient world. Famous historian and agnostic Will Durant points out that if other ancient writings were subjected to the same severe tests of authenticity as have been applied to the New Testament, "a hundred ancient worthies—e.g., Hammurabi, David, Socrates—would fade into legend."[182]

We also know the results of Jesus's life and this body of writing that details it. His immediate followers went into the world with an energy unseen before or since in history, and they went with no governmental authority or military force. Even in the face of opposition from Jewish and Roman authorities, none of those close to him ever recanted his testimony, and none ever alleged any hint of a conspiracy to alter the truth of his witness. Will Durant also made the startling observation:

> *That a few simple men should in one generation have invented so powerful and appealing a personality, so lofty an ethic and so inspiring a vision of human brotherhood, would be a miracle far more incredible than any recorded in the Gospels.*[183]

Albert Schweitzer was one of the first and most sever critics of the historicity of the New Testament. He concluded his great work, *The Quest of the Historical Jesus*, with these words:

> *Jesus means something to our world because a mighty spiritual force streams forth from Him and flows through our time also. This fact can neither be shaken nor confirmed by any historical discovery. It is the solid foundation of Christianity.*[184]

This same spiritual force is evident today and continues to demonstrate the power of the scriptures that have survived as the New Testament.

Summary of Both Testaments

To summarize as simply as possible, Christians have the following general understanding of the Bible: Both Old and New Testaments are the divinely inspired word of God. Both sections of the Bible are valid and supportive of each other. The Old Testament lays the groundwork, explaining the origin and nature of mankind and graphically depicting the inability of men and women, with their God-given freedom of will, to live according to his expectations. The prophets foreshadowed God's plan to rectify this condition. The New Testament reveals the completion of this plan in the life, death, and resurrection of Jesus Christ. Through Jesus human beings are no longer faced with the futile task of working their way to God. A relationship with God, both now and in eternity, is available as a gift. Those who accept this gift today are able to experience a total change in their lives, just like Jesus's first followers and millions more throughout history.

The basic truths presented in the Old and New Testaments are generally obvious, although many passages are complex and open to different interpretations. Scholars tell us there is usually a literal meaning to any passage as well as a deeper moral or spiritual message. This is why it is dangerous to pick out a passage to prove a point. The meaning of any passage usually requires an understanding of the larger context and the deeper meaning. Believers learn that a careful search for the underlying and constant truths of the Bible through study consistently leads to spiritual growth. On the other hand, anyone who just reads this book may have difficulty discerning any significant message for himself or herself.

On this point I can speak from experience. For most of my life, the Bible was just another book. I have found it somewhat analogous to Shakespeare in that a real appreciation requires a good teacher and a lot of study. Most of us study Shakespeare, at least in the beginning, because it is a required subject in high school or college. In the case of the Bible, the most effective motivation for a deeper effort is belief in its divine nature. I hope that from what I have presented so far, my skeptical reader might at least find some cause for wonder. If nothing else I can encourage anyone to look at the Bible with a sense of respect for the great work it is and at least to consider the question: what if this is truly God's word?

PART FOUR

A Skeptic's Favorite Objections

> **Trinity**, n. The traditional threefold divinity worshiped by ambitious Americans: money, sex, and power.[185]

> **Inquisition**, n. An ecclesiastical court for the discouragement of error by mitigating the prevalence and ameliorating the comfort of the erring.[186]

CHAPTER NINETEEN

The Dark Side

A wise guy, or a wise man (depending on your viewpoint), once said, "We expect evil people to do evil, and good people to do good. But when good people do evil, that takes religion."[187] Unfortunately this little barb contains an element of truth. Some terrible things have been done in the name of just about every religion, including Christianity. On one end of the spectrum, we know that Christian nations have fought "holy" wars. On the other end, we hear professed Christians gossiping about each other in church. How can true religion countenance such massive violence and petty hypocrisy?

I do not intend to catalogue or explain every Christian failure. For anyone really interested in this as a subject, a book by Helen Ellerbe titled *The Dark Side of Christian History* is a depressingly comprehensive resource. There are, however, a few noteworthy failures from the past that seem particularly objectionable to modern, well-informed skeptics. I believe that acknowledgment and discussion of these is in order at this point in the narrative.

The Crusades

In November 1095 Pope Urban II called for the First Crusade. With papal blessing and promise of eternal reward, "Christian" armies ventured forth from Europe to the Middle East seeking to liberate the Holy Lands from Muslim domination. These military campaigns and resulting occupations of cities and regions of Palestine went on for almost two hundred years. The bloodshed and violence were of legendary proportions. The motives of the church and many of the crusaders in this "holy" cause were, unfortunately, not always pure. In one sense the crusades brought a new level of power to the church and shifted the attention of warring factions in Europe outward to a common foe. Many of those participating were less motivated by religious zeal than by the prospects of fame and fortune. Today the attitude persists that the Crusades were a misguided or even evil scheme of the early Roman Catholic Church. There is much about this episode in Christian history we can criticize and condemn. However, there is also more to the story.

First, some historical perspective is in order. Islam was founded on the visions of one man: Muhammad ibn Abdullah (AD 570–632), whom Muslims consider God's final prophet. Muhammad led military forces to establish religious and civic control over the Arabian Peninsula before his death. The caliphs who succeeded him continued this program of expansion by force. During the seventh century, Muslim armies conquered Syria, Palestine, Egypt, North Africa, and all of Persia. In the eighth century, this advance continued through Spain and Portugal and into France. In the next hundred years, Sicily and Italy were invaded. Within this brief span of history, Muslim armies conquered all of the Persian Empire and three-quarters of the Christian world.[188]

Early in the eleventh century, Muslim Turks began advancing into Asia Minor. After defeating a Byzantine army at Manzikert in 1071, they conquered most of Anatolia and even threatened Constantinople. In desperation the emperor of the Byzantine Empire appealed to Western Europe and the Roman Pope for aid. Urban II responded to this plea by

THE DARK SIDE

sending forces to relieve Constantinople. He also established a "higher" purpose for the campaign by urging that it continue on to what would be referred to as the Holy Lands.

I do not defend the Crusades, the crusaders, or the church leaders who played roles in the events that followed Pope Urban's call to arms. I will point out, however, that these events have a larger historical context that had been centuries in the making. Warfare was brutal then, as it always has been. Ambition and greed were evidenced on all sides, though they were probably made worse by the religious zeal of the leaders and combatants.

"Why did you become a crusader? You don't even go to church."

Frank Cotham[189]

To me the fundamental evil of the Crusades was the commingling of religion with political, social, and personal causes. This was a human failure. The rulers and religious leaders of the time undoubtedly thought they were doing the right thing. Unfortunately they had the power to act on these beliefs and direct events. There has always been an acute danger of this kind of abuse whenever religious and governmental authorities have been intertwined.

The Inquisition

The Inquisition was an official institution of the Roman Catholic Church charged with the suppression of heresy. First established by papal decree in 1184, local bishops were charged with the duty to combat the spread of new and unsanctioned beliefs that seemed to threaten the church and its interpretation of scripture. On the surface this would seem like a natural function of the church, acting to guard the purity of its own faith and doctrines.

The decentralized approach proved ineffective, however, and was followed by the creation of a professional staff under direction of the Vatican with more-systematic procedures and records. A papal inquisition would go from region to region, solicit testimony about heretical behavior, bring charges, and conduct trials. Punishments consisted of enforced pilgrimages, public recantation, banishment, imprisonment, and, on rare occasion, execution.

This practice was taken to its most horrific and notorious height in Spain under the rule of Ferdinand and Isabella. The Spanish Inquisition was established by papal decree in 1478, but, at the insistence of Ferdinand, was firmly controlled by the Spanish crown. Ferdinand blatantly used the quasi-religious body to promote his most important aim: national unity.[190] Faced with a diversity of religions and cultures, he sought to bring his newly assembled nation together under Catholicism. Jews and Muslims were given the choice of conversion or exile. Thousands left the country in a sad exodus. Those remaining, as well as all other Christians, faced the Inquisition and continuing challenges to the purity and sincerity of their faith.

Organized as a government agency, the Inquisition employed its own professional staff of ecclesiastical and civic officials. The government paid the expenses and benefited from the net income. Tribunals were established in the cities, where informants were encouraged to reveal heretical behaviors of fellow citizens. Evidence was then gathered and trials held in secrecy. Torture was used to gain confessions and information about other offenders. Those found guilty were subject to various punishments, including banishment, imprisonment, and, in extreme cases, public execution by burning. Property and possessions were confiscated, providing a lucrative source of income and corruption.

It is upsetting to read the history of this period and to learn of the inhumanities inflicted on thousands of people because of their "wrong" beliefs. It is especially chilling to consider the fact that many of the inquisitors sincerely believed torture was for the *benefit* of a heretic if it succeeded in saving his soul or the souls of others he might influence.[191] It is practically impossible today to conceive of anyone being so certain of his or her own faith and so fearful of differing cultures and beliefs. Historian Will Durant attempted to explain it this way:

> *Until the middle of the seventeenth century Christians, Jews, and Moslems were more acutely concerned with religion than we are today; their theologies were their most prized and confident possessions; and they looked upon those who rejected these creeds as attacking the foundations of social order and the very significance of human life. Each group was hardened by certainty into intolerance, and branded the others as infidels.*[192]

The fact is unavoidable that the Spanish Inquisition was fueled to a large extent by religious zeal. It is also true, however, that this zeal could have gone only so far without the full power of the state. The king set the agenda and used a vast bureaucratic system to carry it out. Again, human ambition, greed, and jealousy at all levels played their parts in the miserable outcome. Spain did achieve a public conformity of religious practice that endured for centuries. Spain also paid a great price, clinging to a medieval past as the rest of Europe progressed into modernity.

The Crusades and Inquisitions are indeed dark chapters in Christian history. It is difficult for modern Christians to explain or to justify the involvement of the early church in these events. I have concluded these abuses had little to do with Christian belief and instead resulted from human abuses of power. We may feel these Christian leaders should have done better, just as we might expect a better example from Christians today. Unfortunately human beings, including me, have always had difficulty with the simplicity of Jesus's words: "Blessed are the peacemakers." The choice between pacifism and aggressive defense of something we hold to be important has always been difficult. Before I was a Christian, I spent a career in military service devoted to violence in defense of my country. Even now I believe that my service was honorable. I imagine that Pope Urban II and Ferdinand of Spain also considered their actions honorable, even though we may have a very different perspective today.

Again, I believe that the fundamental evil at work here is the use and abuse of religion by those with authority in both the secular and religious realms. The combination of religious and political power was prevalent in the history of Europe until the Protestant Reformation, which at least brought new rivals to the Roman Catholic Church in the sphere of religious authority. Church and state power remained strongly intermingled, however, until the American Revolution. Then, for the first time in history, a nation was founded based on the God-given sanctity of the individual human conscience. As one of the Founding Fathers phrased it, "We have extinguished forever the ambitious hope of making laws for the human mind."[193] Freedom of religion has since become a distinguishing characteristic of most of Western civilization.

Hypocrisy

Earlier in the chapter, I mentioned gossip in church as an example of the petty hypocrisy for which Christians are criticized. We can also see a host of other human failings. Once in a while, we see a visible public failure of a well-known Christian figure such as Jim Bakker or Jimmy Swaggart. We even see scandals involving church leaders abusing children. In these front-page debacles, we learn how self-proclaimed "men of God" can be just as human or even worse than the rest of us. When popes, priests, ministers, and average Christians can't live up to Christ's ideals, how can a nonbeliever take anything of Christianity seriously? What about hypocrisy in the church?

To address this question, I had to first understand what it means to be a Christian. An important step toward accepting Christ's message is a simple understanding of the fact that human beings are imperfect. All people do things they shouldn't do and, especially, fail to do things they should do. All should strive to be better, but it is not through this striving that anyone finds God. Through Jesus God offers a relationship with himself as a gift and requires only that a person accept it. When this happens, God forgives all shortcomings and continues to forgive them as the person tries to perfect this relationship. No Christian can claim to be perfect or even better than any other human being by definition of what it means to be a Christian. They may be weak and prone to failure, but Christians are not prone to hypocrisy. Of all religious people, they are least likely to consider themselves "good" persons.

Even though most Christians accept the fact that they are imperfect human beings in need of God's grace, they face the challenge of living in the world as parents, spouses, and citizens. They don't consider it hypocritical or judgmental to strive for a better society for their families, communities, and nation. This frequently presents a painful dilemma. Can imperfect Christians strive to be Christlike and at the same time stand for a better, more moral world?

They probably can, although obviously a certain amount of caution is in order. Christians know their first duty is to attract nonbelievers to Christ. This is most effective when done through personal example and by sharing Christ's message individually and with humility. How they should go about being good citizens is not so clear. Speaking out against the ills of society may be the right thing to do, but such efforts won't be worth much if those doing the speaking are not above reproach. Even then some will always be accused of being judgmental toward others.

Extra caution is in order when Christians strive to pursue even a righteous agenda through the organized use of political power. When they attempt to legislate morality, the skeptical public is likely to see them and their churches in a poor light. To some extent Christians can accept this. However, such feelings of ill will don't make it easier for them in their appointed mission of winning that public to Christ. Also, Christianity and all other religions have poor track records in the exercise of secular authority. It is no longer possible, if it ever was, to dictate to others in the realm of conscience.

> **Calamity**, n. A more than commonly plain and unmistakable reminder that the affairs of this life are not of our own ordering.[194]

> **Atheist**, n. The ultimate gambler. An evangelist in the church of agnosticism.[195]

CHAPTER TWENTY

Hard Questions

During my long journey as a skeptic, I had my issues with organized religion. First and foremost I thought God should speak to me directly. I could never see the need for ministers or church organizations to interpret for me. I held fast to the thought that he could or should speak to me himself if there were something I needed to know. Even though I waited expectantly (at times), I didn't hear anything. Why did it have to be so difficult to understand his nature or to even *prove* he existed?

As I saw more of the world, I became more conscious of other cultures and religions and found more reason to question the exclusivity of any one spiritual approach. When I directly experienced war-torn areas, natural disasters, poverty, and disease, I wondered still more about my childhood picture of a just and loving god. My questions about these issues went unanswered. I became more agnostic about the idea of a god involved with the world and the lives of human beings, and my skepticism about organized religion grew.

I would like to say I became a Christian because I found the answers to all these questions. However, this was not exactly the way it happened. When I took a step of faith, I still had unanswered questions but made a conscious choice to put some of them aside, at least for that moment. I chose instead to focus on the plain and simple truths I did understand. Since then, and after some years of my winding spiritual journey, I've resolved most of these questions as I have come to see them from a new perspective. I still don't have all the answers, and some of my "insights" might not pass muster with serious theologians. Still, I hope I can give other skeptics some different perspectives on these hard questions.

Why Does It Have to Be So Difficult?

I have asked myself this question many times. As a young person, thanks to my religious upbringing, I was motivated to seek God and to discern what he expected of me in life. This introspective search led me in many directions of inquiry that I have explained in earlier chapters. Even though I learned certain things *about* God, I was continually frustrated in my effort to connect *with* God. My intellectual efforts always seemed to bring me to an impasse. I descended deeper into skepticism and grew more firm in the idea that a loving and personal god would never make it so difficult.

Ironically, I have gone through a very involved process to learn it is not so difficult after all. I have already mentioned an awakening sense of wonder as an important step in my journey. The teachings of Jesus contain specific guidance on this point: "Unless you change and become like little children, you will never enter the kingdom of heaven."[196]

By this, I believe, he did not mean for anyone to forsake his or her intellect. Rather he seemed to be suggesting we look at the world through the eyes of a child, with curiosity and an appropriate sense of wonder. This deceptively simple admonition has profound implications.

Consider the amazing nature of a mother's love, the beauty of a sunset, the ordered complexity of a human cell, the delicate balance of our solar system. We can acquire a lot of information about these phenomena by studying psychology, biology, and astrophysics. However, the deep sense of awe these wonders should inspire comes from a childlike attitude. Such amazement should also stir curiosity about a creator as we appreciate the miraculous nature of the world. The Bible tells us, "The heavens declare the glory of God."[197] In the Bible we also read:

> *What may be known about God is plain to them, because God has made it plain to them. For since the creation of the world God's invisible qualities—his eternal power and divine nature—have been clearly seen, being understood from what has been made, so that men are without excuse.*[198]

A childlike attitude may bring us closer to God. But the question remains: why isn't it easier to understand God? I think we have to accept that he did not intend for it to be easy. We understand from scripture that God made men and women in his own image.[199] I believe that human consciousness represents the essence of what this means. Higher intelligence, creativity, imagination, and initiative are distinct traits not found elsewhere in the natural world. Inherent in these traits are autonomy and freedom of will. The Bible tells us, "God did this so that men would seek him and perhaps reach out for him and find him, though he is not far from each of us."[200] Apparently God put human beings on Earth to live in some form of relationship with him. However, he chose not to enforce this relationship.

Reaching out to God does require an effort. For whatever reason, he chooses not to command our attention or to dictate our thoughts and actions. He has given the world a great body of knowledge about himself, but he is also careful to let each human being find his own way and make his own decisions. Apparently faith in God is meaningless to God without this freedom to choose. He expects us to make an effort to "reach out for him and find him."

For those who diligently seek him, God seems to speak quietly. A revealing Bible story relates how the prophet Elijah looked for God on Mount Horeb. Elijah experienced a great wind that shattered the rocks, an earthquake, and a fire. However, God was not in these violent disturbances. He finally came to Elijah as a "gentle whisper."[201] Through prayer and quiet contemplation, we are most likely to hear God speak directly to our hearts. Those who are most dedicated in their prayer lives seem to be rewarded with a deeper understanding of his nature.

Finally, when considering the difficulty of understanding God, we should at least consider the nature of God and ourselves. If there is an all-knowing, all-powerful entity that created us and all that exists, how much should we expect to understand about him? Obviously he is complex beyond our imagination, and our comprehension is limited. How much does an ant understand a human being?

Even though we wish otherwise, we have to be satisfied with partial glimpses into God's nature and thankful he has given us the resources we have. All we really need to understand is that he is there. If I begin to wonder where he is, I look into the eyes of my children. His miracles, and God himself, are always close at hand.

If There Is a God, Why Do Bad Things Happen?

We know that bad things happen. Children are born every day into conditions of hunger and disease. Natural and manmade disasters occur all over the world regularly. Nations war against each other, and criminals prey on the weak. If there is an all-powerful god and a good god, how can these things happen? Do we have to conclude that either God is not in control or that he is not good?

I heard answers to these questions in the Sunday schools of my youth, but they were not much help:

We are punished for our sins.

If we are punished unfairly in this life, we will receive compensation in the next.

God has his reasons, but we can't understand them.

God is testing us.

God is educating us.

God is forming our character.

I can't deny some element of truth to these assertions. However, from my point of view, occurrences of pain and misfortune seem too random for these explanations. They seem like weak attempts to justify God and to maintain an image of him as all good and all powerful at the same time.

Then there is Satan. As a skeptic, I considered this the weakest answer of all. What are we to think of an unseen, evil creature presiding over the fiery underworld with horns and pitchfork, promoting an agenda of evil in the world? There is no biblical authority for this physical description, but there are many references to a fallen angel, a tempter, a serpent, the beast, the prince of the world, and Satan. The Bible gives a clear picture of Satan as the source of evil in the world. He is depicted as clever and powerful but ultimately no match for God.

Christians believe that Satan is a real figure of the spiritual world, whereas some consider him a concept representing mankind's worst nature. I assume my skeptical reader is happy to leave this question with theologians for now. To me it is obvious that there are times when we are almost overwhelmed by the sense of an evil force or forces in the world that confront decency at every turn. Those who trade in drugs, pornography, and terrorism all target the innocent in pursuit of their agendas of destruction. Sometimes evil seems disturbingly well-organized and purposeful.

"This is the part of religion we could do without."

Frank Cotham[202]

I believe the most important truth about evil and misfortune in the world is that God does not cause it. The greatest source of human suffering is what humans do to each other. As I have already stated, the fact that we are created in God's image means we have the capability to make choices in life. Sometimes we make bad choices due to laziness, ignorance, or greed. We harm others. God does not usually intervene.

The other source of suffering is the process of natural forces on the planet. Movement of the Earth's crust, winds, rain, and tides all work according to natural laws. Bacteria and viruses live and grow according to their biological necessities. I do not believe that God directs the paths of hurricanes or spreads germs in particular patterns. This is not to say he can't do these things or can't respond to prayer. But I believe he *normally* allows the world to function according to the natural laws he set in place.

Death is an event that eventually overtakes every living thing in accordance with God's plan for the natural world. Even though we sometimes think we would like to live forever, the world would unfortunately become a pretty crowded place. In literature those who cannot die are seen as tragic figures. The inevitability of death seems to give life its meaning and urgency.

When death occurs suddenly and unexpectedly, we often consider it tragic and wonder why God allows such apparent injustice. Again, we have to look to natural forces or human agents acting wrongly or carelessly. Christians have a special peace about this subject, knowing where they are going when life is over, whatever the cause. When a Christian family has a death, the question can be asked: who should be mourned, the one who died, or the ones left behind?

The main point about bad things is that God does not cause them to happen. He also does not promise to shield us from them. What he does promise is that he will be with us through whatever happens:

> *Neither death nor life, neither angels nor demons, neither the present nor the future, nor any powers, neither height nor depth, nor anything else in all creation, will be able to separate us from the love of God that is in Christ Jesus our Lord.*[203]

The ultimate freedom that cannot be taken away from any human being is the freedom to choose one's attitude toward any situation. If we refuse to be depressed or defeated then neither is inevitable. If we choose to be hopeful and optimistic, we are likely to work our way out of any problem. I don't mean to make this sound easy. There are true disasters in life that make it virtually impossible to find such an attitude within ourselves. The only source of such strength is God. If we are able to turn to God in a crisis, hope and peace of mind are always available. In fact if we can look at our problems as opportunities to deepen our relationship with God, there is no problem without potential for good. A crisis may have no meaning in itself, but we can give it meaning by what we do in response to it.

Is There Only One Way?

I mentioned a body of knowledge about God. The question automatically follows: what constitutes this body of knowledge? Does it include the Vedas and Upanishads of Hinduism, the Dhammapada of Buddhism, the Quran of Islam, and the Bible of Judaism and Christianity? In other words do all the world's religions contain elements of truth about God? Or is there a single truth?

To the modern skeptic, this is undoubtedly the most formidable question affecting his or her search for spiritual understanding. It is also the most-cited problem with Christianity, which asserts it is *the only way* to God. Is this a form of religious arrogance or some holdover from the absolute beliefs of medieval times? Can a modern person still hold such a "narrow" view?

Even though Christians are certain Jesus is the way to God, I don't think anyone can be too confident in his or her knowledge of God's ultimate plan for all mankind. I don't think any Christian can confidently assert that God has made no provision for good Hindus, Muslims, or others who have not heard of Jesus Christ. An Episcopal priest once told me that Christianity is like Interstate 95. From South Carolina it is the best and most direct route to Washington, DC. There may be other ways to get there, but these routes may be longer, slower, more difficult, and less certain. There may be detours, dead ends, and the potential for getting lost. We know that we can *definitely* get to Washington on I-95.[204] There is also Episcopal liturgy in *The Book of Common Prayer* asking God to bless "all who have died in the communion of your Church, and those whose faith is known to you alone."[205] These provisions for apparent nonbelievers may not be acceptable to all Christian theologians, but they do seem to be clear reminders that we don't understand *everything* about God's plans for the world he made.

I would, however, caution anyone who comfortably thinks he or she is one of those "good" people who God will "take care of" in the end. How many good Hindus, Muslims, atheists, or Christians are there? I suppose it depends on whose definition of good we are using. Yours may be more lenient than mine. We both may be more lenient than God. The Bible tells us, "All fall short of the glory of God."[206] How many selfish, thoughtless, or evil things can a person do and still be good? This is a matter of conscience between every individual and God. As my doubts have grown about how good a person I am, I have found myself on unexpected common ground with practically every Christian I have met.

This leads to a very important difference I have found between Christianity and the other major religions of the world. Most religions require that human beings become good by working their way toward some form of perfection. Heaven or spiritual fulfillment has to be earned through a process. The Buddhist works his way along the Eightfold Path to reach nirvana. The Hindu expects many lifetimes of self-improvement to attain enlightenment. Muslims submit to God by adhering to the Five Pillars of Islam. Jews try to conform to God's law as provided in the Old Testament. This law became more elaborate over the centuries until even the experts became confused over the rules of daily living. Rules and rituals in Jewish and most other cultures became barriers to God rather than a clear path.

Christians believe that Jesus Christ reestablished the path to God for *all* of humanity. The essence of his message is reconciliation and forgiveness. Through him the need for all other mediators, sacrifices, and rituals is removed. No one is good enough by his or her own efforts, and Jesus offers himself to bridge the gap. A close and personal relationship with God is thus presented as a gift available at any moment to every human being.

If you are like me, the issue of Christian exclusivity has been a significant barrier to further investigation. I hope this discussion gives you something to think about. It may be tempting to throw up your hands at the multiplicity of religions in the world and at the apparent futility of sorting it all out. For me this was an easy way to avoid considering the truth or even the meaning of the Christian message.

Christians believe that the gospel message bears the truth about God and how we are to live in relationship with him. Is this the one and only truth? I can only offer my experience and a preview of the next few chapters. By making a decision to accept this message, I felt God's presence in my life for the first time. This new relationship has brought me true peace in my present life and hope for the next. Is it arrogant to want to share this message with others? It may seem so, and this is the dilemma Christians face. Christ admonished his followers to "Feed my sheep."[207] He didn't say *force*-feed them or compel them in any way. There may be no room for pressure or arrogance, but there should be a sense of urgency about such life-changing news.

PART FIVE

A New Journey

> Skepticism, like chastity, should not be relinquished too readily.
> —George Santayana[208]

> Skeptical scrutiny is the means in both Science and Religion by which deep thoughts can be winnowed from deep nonsense.
> —Carl Sagan[209]

CHAPTER TWENTY-ONE

A Skeptic's Worst Moment

After these winding detours through the landscapes of science, scripture, and troubling questions, it's time to return to the more personal part of my spiritual journey as we draw nearer to what I tentatively call a "destination." Even though this is not the entirely appropriate word, I am obviously trying to get to the main point of this book and a resolution of my own and other skeptics' spiritual doubts. So we return to my quasi-autobiography, anticipating at least some significant stopping point not too far ahead.

The reader may recall the difficulties, recounted earlier, that I experienced in dealing with the deaths of loved ones. Throughout that time I continued to cling "religiously" to a lifelong skeptical outlook. In the Sunday school of my early life, I had learned the Bible verse, "Blessed are the poor in spirit."[210] This statement, made by Jesus, never made sense to me until a time arrived in my marriage when I saw my wife struggle with the death of her mother.

During this critical time, Lani dealt with her pain by seeking comfort in a women's Bible study. She was invited by a friend and found that she enjoyed the fellowship and daily lessons. I could see that she was having a positive experience with new thoughts and ideas. From a very low point in her life, and even because of it, I saw her open up to something new. She began to emerge from the bad time and adopt a more positive attitude. She was taking many of her Bible lessons to heart. I thought the effects of this were mostly wonderful, but I also had the disturbing thought that we were moving in different intellectual directions for the first time in our marriage.

Then something rather un-Episcopalian happened to us at our church. Some friends asked us to go on a weekend retreat. They and others in the church had already been to Cursillo and insisted we would enjoy it.[211] I was not thrilled about the prospect, but Lani was. So again we used our time-tested family decision-making formula and did what Lani wanted to do. No one told me too much about it, which was a very good thing; I would have fought harder not to go.

A lot of things happened to me on that weekend, much of it painful. It started with a nightlong silent retreat dedicated to introspection. During the rest of the weekend, even as other activities were taking place, this state of inward focus continued and deepened. It was not easy for me to admit to myself that I had problems of any kind since so many tangible aspects of my life were in such good shape. Gradually, however, all my worries and unanswered questions came churning up to a conscious level. For the first time, I considered my lack of purpose and enthusiasm in a spiritual light. I became conscious of a spiritual void within myself that had likely been there all my life, though masked for years by near-religious dedication to my professional life. Most important of all, I began to accept the fact that my questions were not going to be answered through my own intellectual thought processes.

In one of the weekend sessions, someone made the point that God places an emptiness within us that only he can fill, and he has offered us the means to fill it in the form of a gift. However, a gift is not a gift unless it is *received*. In other words a gift from God is meaningless as a *concept* and becomes meaningful only if we accept it individually and personally.

In earlier chapters I mentioned a change in my outlook as I began to consider the miraculous nature of the natural world. This new perspective assumed a sharper focus during this retreat as I looked more carefully at the Bible verse I have already mentioned: "Unless you change and become like little children, you will never enter the kingdom of heaven."[212] Did this imply unquestioning acceptance of religious authority or simply a deeper sense of wonder about God? I wasn't sure of the answer at that moment, but I did know that the least likely adjective for my attitude toward life at that time was *childlike*.

During the weekend there was a lot of talk about Jesus Christ. I seemed to hear it from a distance, as I really wasn't ready for more confusion in my mental state. In my intellectual landscape, he was a great ethics teacher who was killed for going against the Jewish establishment of his time. I was taught in Sunday school that he "died for our sins." This was never meaningful to me since the idea of sin was not meaningful. As a young person, I never felt sinful, and the idea of original sin seemed preposterous. I believed more in Ayn Rand's assertion that this idea was a religious trick to keep mankind in a state of guilt. I didn't know about sin, but I knew a lot about guilt. I was not ready to connect those dots. I filed this subject away in my mind for another day.[213]

Another day came only weeks later. I returned from the weekend retreat in an exhausted, somewhat euphoric state of mind. I knew I had to get back to the real world, and I did not want to start overanalyzing my confusing insights. I did pick up the Bible a few times, turning mainly to the New Testament, and I even paid more attention in church. I talked about all this with Lani, and she wisely let me stumble on with my thoughts. I also accepted an invitation from a good friend to attend a breakfast meeting and talk by a former astronaut. I didn't realize at the time that this was to be a prayer breakfast.

In September 1993 the first Gathering of Men was held in Myrtle Beach, South Carolina. The speaker for the occasion was Charles Duke, the well-known Apollo 13 astronaut and moonwalker. I enjoyed the stories about his life and experiences in space. I identified with his perspectives as a military man, such as his encounter with an air force pay clerk when he tried to collect a mileage allowance for his trip to the moon. I started squirming in my seat, however, when he began to slip into spiritual matters.

Charlie Duke proceeded to give what I have since learned was a witness talk for Jesus Christ. This was not a theological argument or a cataloging of proofs. It was simply a statement of what had happened to the former astronaut in his life. It was hard not to listen to a respected military man who seemed to be talking directly to me.

He used a word over and over that resonated in my mind. That word was *decision*. He made the point that sooner or later we each must make a decision about Jesus: either he was the Son of God as he proclaimed, or he was the biggest liar and fraud in history. The Bible allows no intermediate interpretation, such as sage or prophet. Considering the historical importance of Christianity as a religion and its influence in the world, this is an extremely important decision on a personal level. This matter deserves investigation and careful consideration. Ignoring the decision is a decision in itself.

Finally Duke said, "Men, you each have to weigh the pros and cons for yourselves. However, you can't go on weighing the pros and cons forever." This was an especially powerful statement to me since I had gone through a similar thought process about marriage, which I have already described. Feelings change in romantic relationships, whereas true love requires a decision. I have always been thankful for that insight. Now a man I respected and with whom I strongly identified was presenting me with another very important decision. At that moment, I felt the need to let go of the skepticism and doubt that had been such important parts of my nature for so long.

At that moment I didn't know everything about Jesus. However, I did know some things. I knew about his life and teachings, as I have already described, and I knew about the effect he had on countless people throughout history. Some of them were even friends of mine whom I respected. I was aware of much of the information I have related through the course of this book. At that time I felt I knew enough to make a decision to accept this evidence as sufficient proof that Jesus was and is the Son of God.

I joined in a simple prayer, asking Jesus to come into my heart and take charge of my life. I was very conscious of the need to put my skepticism on hold for that time and instead to *come as a child*. I focused on the simplicity of Christ's message and the reality of a love that put a former astronaut in front of me that morning. I accepted this gift and took that first small step Charlie Duke asked me to take: trusting in Jesus to take charge of my life and help me go in a new direction—toward him.

> Mystery creates wonder, and wonder is the basis of man's desire to understand.
> —Neil Armstrong[214]

> Take the first step in faith. You don't have to see the whole staircase, just take the first step.
> —Dr. Martin Luther King Jr.[215]

CHAPTER TWENTY-TWO

The Anatomy of a Step of Faith

I hope the details of my journey presented so far serve a purpose. I have tried to illustrate the lengths to which I have gone in my intellectual travels to find answers to life's important questions. I know that your journey is different, and your perspectives are not the same as mine. Even so, I assume we are on the same search.

I have shared this material about my life for one purpose: to explain the circumstances leading to a small step of faith on my part. This is the crux of my story. I feel that this step was not the culmination of an information-gathering process even though information and knowledge have always been important to me. A new fact did not finally cause a light to go on. My step of faith involved a decision to believe. I came to a point on my tortuous path where I thought I knew enough to make such a decision. Taking the step was more a matter of acceptance, of letting go, than of reaching some brilliant conclusion. The most compelling aspect of this that I can share with you is the fact that it turned out to be the best thing I have done in my life.

THE ANATOMY OF A STEP OF FAITH

I have written this book because I hope you will make the same decision. I, of all people, know how difficult this is. When I say I knew enough, I speak only for myself. My family and cultural history and my whole process of inquiry came together to suggest to me that I knew enough. But what about you?

Because you are a fellow skeptic, I know you are hard to convince. Taking such a step may be difficult because you think you don't know enough or because you know *too much*. You may still be confused about the nature of God and uncertain about his involvement in human history and your life. You may still have questions about the Bible, and there may be theological issues that have not been resolved.

I know I haven't answered every question, even though I hope I have helped remove some of your barriers to thinking about a spiritual life. I have presented a lot of information, and it is difficult to know how much is enough. But I have also tried to make an important point: information will get you only so far in your search. You shouldn't expect an answer to every question.

A step of faith does not have to be difficult. Every time you get into a car, you put your faith in the designs of the steering, braking, and airbag systems, about which you know little. On an airliner you put your faith in a pilot you've never met. You take the history-book accounts of ancient civilizations as fact. You believe that your wife loves you. Yet in spiritual matters, you demand airtight proof before you will believe anything. Maybe some lesser accumulation of reasonable evidence should be adequate. In your search there should come a time when you know enough to take a step. The benefits are incalculable. I have never met anyone who regrets having taken a step of faith toward God.

> **Decide**, v. To succumb to the preponderance of one set of disasters over another set.[216]

> I believe that belief gives you a direction in the confusion. But you don't see the full picture. That's the point. That's what faith is.
> —Bono of U2[217]

CHAPTER TWENTY-THREE

Decisions, Decisions

Life Decisions

There are certain questions in life that we can't avoid. For example, we have to decide sooner or later how we're going to make a living. A fortunate few figure this out early in life. Most of us, however, need years in the educational system and even some trial and error to evaluate career choices. This can go on for a long time. There comes a point, however, or at least there should, when a decision is necessary. A decision requires a commitment to a definite, long-range course of action. If no decision is made, there may be no immediate repercussions. No decision, however, is a prescription for drift and lack of success. With no decision we have little chance of mastering the tools of any trade.

As I have already mentioned, I see a similar process at work between members of the opposite sex. At some point in life, most begin to perceive the need for a long-term mate. A lot of people seem to work on the basis of their feelings and the expectation that they will just *know* when the right person comes along. They expect to fall in love. I don't discount the reality of falling in love, because I did so. However,

I don't think that feelings of love are a dependable basis for a long-term relationship.

Along with our emotions, there needs to be a degree of objectivity. This requires an information-gathering process. For some this process can go on for a long time. Again, there comes a point when a decision is required. We may *fall* in love, but we have to *decide* that we're going to commit to a lasting relationship. I believe that this is one of the most profound decisions we ever make because it affects not only our own lives but the lives of future children and extended families. For this reason it is and should be difficult to make. Not deciding may work for a long time. However, this ensures a relationship that is vulnerable to disagreements and conflict. A long-lasting relationship requires a decision to do whatever it takes to make it through difficult times. This commitment is the essential difference between marriage and "living together."

There is a distinct parallel to this need for decision in the area of our lives where we long to find meaning and purpose. There is a tendency to believe that the process of living will eventually lead to some form of truth with which we can live. Although some go about this systematically, many more seem to have no pressing concern about reaching any final resolution in this area. The exigencies of life frequently crowd out concerns about the long-range future, especially the eternal future. There are always more-pressing problems. Not resolving the so-called *big picture* affects different people in different ways.

Outwardly most people give the appearance of living peaceful, contented lives, and for a fortunate few this is actually the case. Most of us, however, find our lives filled to varying degrees with guilt and ill-defined anxieties that we cope with in a variety of ways. Some of us try to work harder at our jobs or in our roles as spouses, parents, or friends. Some become immersed in hobbies and entertainment. Others with more-acute stress turn to counseling and self-improvement programs. At the extreme end, there are those facing severe crises in their lives leading to depression and more-destructive "remedies," such as drinking and drugs.

Anxiety, depression, and guilt are often based on very real problems, and I don't want to minimize them. I believe, however, that these human conditions reflect an underlying reality: without God there is little chance anyone will experience true peace in his or her life. This is the spiritual issue that every person must face. I have heard it said and I am convinced it is true: "Every person has a void in his or her heart that only God can fill." This is an accurate description of the human condition. Sometimes we are not conscious of the void. Sometimes we are only vaguely aware of it during our anxious and fearful moments. Sometimes it is acutely obvious when we are filled with guilt, anger, or remorse.

Anyone who considers himself a seeker is conscious of the need for something missing in his or her life. My skeptical reader, however, is probably resistant to the idea of a *spiritual* void. Like me you want to look everywhere else for answers. Our nature fights against framing any problem in other than objective terms. We want to solve problems with new facts and more information. When nothing changes, however, we have to consider another approach.

I have already mentioned the comedian who exhorted his audiences, "Don't tell me your doubts…Tell me what you believe in!"[218] This comment bothered me when I heard it because it forced me to admit something to myself. I realized that even though I knew a lot about comparative religion, philosophy, and science, I still had only doubts to share with others. New information has always been important to me, as I believe it is for any skeptical person. However, learning more about these subjects did not lead me to *belief* in anything. I gained more knowledge, but my doubts remained. All my ill-defined anxieties also remained. I know from experience how easy it is to focus on those doubts.

Another Kind of Decision

I would like to ask now for my skeptical reader's careful attention. So far this book has been another information-gathering foray in your search

DECISIONS, DECISIONS

for understanding. You have undoubtedly already spent years in the pursuit of knowledge and answers to your questions. I believe it is important for you to realize that your ultimate answer is not likely to come from additional information. All your doubts will never be satisfied. Your answer will come when you make a decision about what you already know.

You have probably found attractive certain aspects of Eastern religions, ancient and modern philosophy, new age mysticism, scientific naturalism, and your own thoughts. I don't want to argue against any source of knowledge you hold as important for yourself. However, I assume you are continuing to seek more meaningful answers.

In the past you may have been ambivalent or even antagonistic about Christianity. I hope I have been effective in giving you a new perspective. Christianity is not another self-help program with a list of things you must do to be a better person. You do not have to become a better person to belong. It is not based on rules and regulation. Christians do not consider themselves better than anyone else. They know instead that they are fallen human beings. They consider Jesus Christ the expression of God's love for mankind and the fulfillment of God's plan to give every human being the opportunity to live in relationship with him in this life and in the eternal future.

By living in a Christian-based culture and by learning from many sources, including this book, you know quite a lot about Jesus and his message. You know what is proclaimed about him in scripture—that he was the Son of God who came into the world as a humble servant, healer, and teacher; that he suffered and died to pay the price for the failures of humanity; that he was resurrected from the dead and commissioned his followers to carry forth the most important message in history to the world—that in love God has given his son as the way to him. Through Jesus mankind no longer has to be separated from God because of what they have done or failed to do.

You know also that Jesus was an extraordinary teacher and leader who energized a core group of followers to carry this message to the known world two thousand years ago. This message eventually affected the lives of billions of human beings and became the basis of the world's most widespread religion. This religion is a foundational element of practically every institution of Western civilization and was probably important to the family lives of most of your ancestors. Jesus's importance as a historical figure alone makes him worthy of your serious attention.

The Life-or-Death Decision

I ask you now to consider Jesus Christ and these claims about him. You have this information and know his effect on history. You have undoubtedly weighed this information and considered the pros and cons for and against him. His words do not leave room for you to decide that he was just a great teacher. He offers you a gift of incalculable value—a relationship with God. There may be more to learn about him, but there will be no end to that process. You can't go on weighing the pros and cons forever. At some point you must make a decision. I strongly suspect you know enough to do so now.

In talking with you about your spiritual condition, some Christians might ask you a question at this point: if you were to die today, could you say for certain that you would go to heaven?[219] If you hope you will or think you might, or if you honestly don't know, you need to realize there is one way to be certain. A decision *for* Jesus is that way. It is also the sure path to a new life now. A personal relationship with God is possible in this life as well as in eternity. I offer my personal assurance again that my life changed when I made this decision, and I have met no one who regrets having made this decision for himself or herself.

A decision for Jesus Christ means you are ready to move this knowledge about him from your head to your heart. For now you may have to defer your skeptical nature to some extent and come as a child. You will need to acknowledge him as the Son of God and as the Lord of your life. This means you are ready to follow him and to allow him to direct your life. In other words you are ready to receive him into your heart.

You can make this decision for Jesus right now. If you are able to put your skeptical nature on hold for now and accept Jesus into your heart for who he claims to be, I urge you to say the following prayer. I assure you God is listening.

> *Lord Jesus, I acknowledge you as my Lord and Savior. Forgive me for all the ways I have disappointed you and others in my life. I receive you into my heart. Please come into my life now and take charge of my life. Thank you, Lord, for this precious gift. Amen.*

If you have prayed this prayer, I suggest you sit for a while in quiet contemplation. Continue to talk to God about what you have done. Listen. He is there. He promises you that, "The peace of God, which transcends all understanding, will guard your heart and your mind in Christ Jesus."[220]

I prayed this prayer for the first time in 1993. Although once was enough, I repeat it now just about every day. I have to report that at the time I first said it, I did not experience a blinding light or voice from heaven welcoming me into the fold. I did, however, experience an inner peace unlike anything before in my life. I was able to talk to God sincerely for the first time. Scripture came to life. I looked at other people in a new light. From that moment my confidence grew that I was on the right path to finding my true purpose in life.

If you have said this prayer for the first time or repeated it after saying something similar a long time ago, I promise you God welcomes you and blesses your decision. Every believer also welcomes you as a new Christian. You have taken the step of faith that places you on a new path in life as of this moment.

The next and final chapter will have suggestions about your spiritual journey and search for purpose. Right now there are a few simple steps I urge you to take:

1. Share what you have done with another person, preferably a Christian friend or clergyman. See if this person will meet with you at least once a week for the next month. Ask for advice and counsel.

2. Dust off the Bible you have somewhere. Read the following passages:
    a. Colossians 1:15–23. Christ has reconciled you to God.
    b. Ephesians 3:12. You can approach God with freedom and confidence.
    c. 2 Corinthians 5:17. You are truly a new creation.
    d. Romans 8:14–17. With Christ you are a child and heir of God.
    e. John 3:16. Through Christ you are a very special person. Read this familiar passage, substituting your name for "the world" and "whoever."

3. Attend a church service. Make this the first step in finding a church where you feel truly at home. You need other Christians, and they need you.

4. Talk to God. In other words, pray. Praise him, share your concerns, ask for his direction and protection.

5. Be patient with yourself. You will want to please God, but he is not waiting for you to become a better person. God loves you now. You have joined his family. He will help you move forward.

> I just say to you, what's important to us? To be in prayer, Bible study, and certainly seeking out those Godly mentors that we think are walking right next to the Lord.
>
> —Joe Gibbs[221]

> Preach the Gospel at all times and when necessary use words.
>
> —Francis of Assisi[222]

CHAPTER TWENTY-FOUR

Beyond Nice

The best description I have heard of the Christian life is that it is a "journey." Some talk about their "walk" with Christ. What you should try to picture is movement. You are going somewhere. You are directing your path toward God. You want to know him, and you want to please him. You can do both to a degree, but in this lifetime you are probably not going to do either completely. You will have a sense of direction, but you will not likely reach a final destination. There will always be new horizons ahead.

Some parts of the journey will be smooth and effortless, others difficult. Sometimes God will seem close. Sometimes he will seem far away. You will undoubtedly need help as you travel. God's promise to you is that he will be with you. Your efforts and his grace will bring you ever closer.

Your spiritual journey as a new Christian will be more rewarding than anything you have experienced. You will learn the distinguishing feature of his kingdom: "God is love."[223]

As this fundamental truth takes hold in your life, your image of yourself and others will change. You will be less anxious about your life. You will see others in a more sympathetic light. You will interact with fellow Christians on a deeper and more meaningful level. As you seek God in prayer, study, and service, your spiritual horizons will expand.

Bookstores are full of how-to books on the Christian life. I haven't read most of them, but I know there are many good ones. One of my favorite writers is John Eldridge. In his widely read book *Wild at Heart*, he separates his approach from most others' by pointedly *not* giving a list of things to do. There is more to being a Christian than just being a *nice* person. There is a need for passion and boldness. His images are inspiring. For men there are battles to fight and adventures to live. Women are called to be what they were meant to be: the crown of creation.[224] As I have struggled to figure out my mission in God's service, this higher vision has been very motivating. Whether our tasks of the moment are exciting or mundane, our spiritual growth and service to God are part of a great and ultimately meaningful adventure.

Next to the Bible, one of the all-time best-selling books for Christians has been *The Purpose Driven Life* by Rick Warren. This book is the basis of a small group program called 40 Days of Purpose that has been used by countless churches around the nation, mine included. I have had the opportunity to lead groups through this curriculum. This book also does not give you more things to do. Its aim is to *simplify* your life by helping you focus on what is most important. I recommend you put *The Purpose Driven Life* at the top of your reading list. You will learn about God's purpose for you in these essential areas:

1. *Living closer to God.*
2. *Loving other believers.*
3. *Becoming more like Jesus Christ.*
4. *Serving others.*
5. *Helping others to begin new lives.*

A Christian friend once explained to me the difference between "church work" and the "work of the church."[225] The former goes on inside the church, the latter outside. The first four items on the list above generally pertain to your spiritual growth and service within the church. Each of these is a rewarding pursuit that will add new meaning to your life, and each is essential to your progress.

The work of the church goes on outside the church. As your life changes, you will feel the need to share what you have experienced with others. I hesitate to use the word *evangelism* here because many have a wrong impression about it. For many, preaching on street corners and at tent revivals comes to mind. We don't need a label to understand that sharing the gospel with others is an important purpose for every Christian.

Fortunately, few are called to preach on street corners or in distant lands. In fact few are called to preach at all. We all have opportunities, however, to share God's love in our homes, places of work, and social settings. We do this mainly by example, through our actions toward family members, friends, and associates. We listen, love, and serve. The deeper relationships that result are invariably good for our families, offices, and communities. Occasionally we get opportunities to share our own spiritual stories. There is never a cause for argument when you simply set forth what has happened in your life. When the time is right, this can be very meaningful to someone with whom you have already established a close relationship.

I believe that this personal interaction is the most meaningful manifestation of the Christian life for most Christians. However, I don't want to discourage anyone from more-arduous service. There are obviously many ways to contribute to the growth of God's kingdom. Some people are called specifically to evangelical and missionary fields. Many others find ways to support and encourage those engaged in this work. Some are called into the political arena. Many are extremely purposeful in their support of charitable causes, especially those reflecting the outreach efforts of their churches. I was tempted to write at this point that you are limited only by your interests, imagination, and opportunities. However, you are actually not limited at all. A wise Christian said, "God does not call the qualified. He qualifies those he calls." Scripture clearly reminds us, "With God all things are possible."[226]

I recommend once again to be patient with yourself in your journey. With so much to learn and do, it can sometimes be overwhelming. This can be true especially of life in a church. There will be endless opportunities for service and learning. I encourage you to get involved, but I will also give you a biblical reminder: "For we are God's workmanship, created in Christ Jesus to do good works, which God prepared in advance for us to do."[227] There is much good work to be done. However, you aren't expected to do it all. In time you will discover how you can best serve God by doing the things he has in mind for you. This will require an effort on your part as you learn more about your gifts and the opportunities that are available. It will undoubtedly take some trial and error. When you are truly doing the work God has prepared for you, it will not be a burden.

My journey since coming to Christ has had its twists and turns. As I pondered my role as a new Christian, a friend advised me to get involved in something and do the obvious tasks that presented themselves. Lani and I did this by faithfully supporting the Cursillo ministry, which I mentioned earlier, for a number years as team members and leaders.

As we helped others grow spiritually, we grew steadily in our faith. The many hours and extended travel were never burdens to either of us.

My life as a Christian changed completely on a day in 1998 as I was driving my car, listening to a book on tape about the American Revolution. Since childhood, military history has been a passionate interest, heightened further by my career in military service. Being familiar with the precarious outcomes of many battles, I had for some time thought of writing a book about the role of luck in war. On that day, however, as I listened to the description of an incident that changed the outcome of the Battle of Trenton, God seemed to speak directly to me. I felt washed from head to toe by the sudden insight that *this* incident was not luck but was rather the hand of God saving the remnant of the Continental Army and the American Revolution. In 2001 I published my first book, *God in the Trenches*, detailing this and other miraculous events that turned the tide in America's favor when her survival was at stake.

While praying, researching, and writing this and other books, I found the central purpose of my life in service to God's kingdom. Since then, with the support of my family and a great publisher, I have continued to write and speak about God's hand in history and the power of faith during wartime. As a former skeptic, I have always kept the doubtful at the forefront of my thoughts, writing specifically for skeptics with a questioning mind-set similar to my own.

Finally, I would like to offer one more bit of advice for you in your journey ahead. It is an important biblical reminder about where we stand with God: "For it is by grace you have been saved, through faith—and this not from yourselves, it is the gift of God—not by works, so that no one can boast."[228] If you and I are safely in Jesus's fold and members of God's kingdom, it is by *his* grace.

I have put great emphasis in this book on the need for a decision about Jesus. This is a step each of us must take for ourselves. However, it is God who makes it even possible. He sent his son. He gave us his word. He gives us the opportunity to hear and believe. He allows our ears and eyes to open. There is truly no room for pride in making this decision. We can only be grateful that we have a loving and forgiving God who, in his power and majesty, somehow reaches out to us, giving us the opportunity to come to him, to be part of his kingdom, and to do his work in the world. Just remember, you are not working your way to God. You are already there. He loves you now. He does not need for you to do things for him. *You* have a need to serve God. It is in this service that you will find the true meaning and purpose of your life.

> **Expert**, n. A person who avoids small error as he sweeps on to the grand fallacy.[229]

> A room without books is like a body without a soul.
> —Cicero[230]

BIBLIOGRAPHY

Audesirk, Gerald and Teresa Audesirk. *Biology: Life on Earth*, 2nd Edition. New York: Macmillan Publishing Company, 1989.

Barnes-Svarney, Patricia. *New York Public Library Science Desk Reference.* New York: Macmillan/Stonesong Press Book, 1995.

Barrow, John D. *Theories of Everything: The Quest for Ultimate Explanation.* Oxford: Clarendon Press, 1991.

Bayan, Rick. *The Cynic's Dictionary.* Edison, New Jersey: Castle Books, 2002.

Better, Nancy M. "Midlife Madness." *More Magazine*, May 2005.

Bierce, Ambrose. *The Enlarged Devil's Dictionary.* New York: Doubleday and Company, Inc., 1967.

Borg, Marcus J. *Jesus in Contemporary Scholarship.* Valley Forge, Pennsylvania: Trinity Press International, 1994.

Britannica, *The New Encyclopedia Britannica, 15th Edition,* Vol. 18. London, Chicago: Encyclopedia Brittanica, Inc., 2005.

Bureau of the Census. *Statistical Abstract of the United States: 1998* (118th Edition). Washington, DC: US Bureau of the Census, 1998.

Cambridge University. *The Cambridge Encyclopedia of Earth Sciences.* New York: Crown Publishers/Cambridge University Press, 1981.

Capra, Fritjof. *The Hidden Connections: Integrating the Biological, Cognitive, and Social Dimensions of Life into a Science of Sustainability.* New York: Doubleday, 2002.

Carroll, Robert Todd. *The Skeptic's Dictionary.* John Wiley and Sons, 1994–2006. Also see http://skepdic.com.

Collins, Francis S. *The Language of God: A Scientist Presents Evidence for Belief.* New York: Free Press, 2006.

Darwin, Charles. *The Origin of Species by Means of Natural Selection*, Vols. I and II. New York: D. Appleton & Company, 1915.

Dawkins, Richard. *The Blind Watchmaker.* New York: WW Norton & Company, 1986.

Dawkins, Richard. *The Selfish Gene.* Oxford and New York: Oxford University Press, 1976.

Dembski, William A. *The Design Revolution: Answering the Toughest Questions About Intelligent Design.* Downers Grove, Illinois: InterVarsity Press, 2004.

Durant, Will. *Caesar and Christ. The Story of Civilization, Vol. III.* New York: Simon & Schuster, 1944.

Durant, Will. *The Reformation. The Story of Civilization, Vol. VI.* New York: Simon & Schuster, 1957.

Ehrman, Bart D. *The Historical Jesus.* Chantilly, Virginia: The Teaching Company, 2000.

Eiselen, Frederick C., Edwin Lewis, and David C. Downey, eds. *The Abingdon Bible Commentary.* New York, Nashville: Abingdon Press, 1929.

Feynman, Richard P. *The Meaning of It All: Thoughts of a Citizen Scientist.* Reading, Massachusetts: Addison-Wesley, 1998.

Fischler, Martin A. and Oscar Firschein. *Intelligence: The Eye, the Brain, and the Computer.* Reading, Massachusetts: Addison-Wesley, 1987.

Fitzgerald, Edward, trans. *The Rubáiyát of Omar Khayyám.* New York: The Illustrated Editions Company, 1938.

BIBLIOGRAPHY

Fuller, Robert C. *Spiritual but Not Religious: Understanding Unchurched America.* Oxford: Oxford University Press, 2001.

Gould, Stephen Jay. *Dinosaur in a Haystack: Reflections in Natural History.* New York: Harmony Books, 1995.

Gould, Stephan Jay. "Evolution's Erratic Pace." *Natural History,* Vol. 86, No.5, May 1977.

Hawking, Stephen. *A Brief History of Time.* New York: Bantam Books, 1988.

Hawking, Stephen. *Black Holes and Baby Universes.* New York: Bantam Books, 1993.

Helfaer, Philip M. *The Psychology of Religious Doubt.* Boston: Beacon Press, 1972.

Jastrow, Robert. *God and the Astronomers.* New York and London: WW Norton & Company, 1992.

Josephus, Flavius. *The Antiquities of the Jews.* From *The Works of Flavius Josephus,* translated by William Whiston, London: Chatto & Windus 1912.

Keller, Werner. *The Bible as History*, 2nd Revised Edition. New York: William Morrow, 1980.

Kennedy, D. James. *Evangelism Explosion: The Coral Ridge Program for Lay Witness.* Wheaton, Illinois: Tyndale House Publishers, 1983.

Kushner, Harold S. *When Bad Things Happen to Good People.* New York: Avon Books, 1981.

Madden, Thomas F. *"God Wills It!": Understanding the Crusades.* Recorded Books, 2005.

Maslow, Abraham. *Motivation and Personality.* New York: Harper & Row, 1970.

Mazar, Amihai. *Archaeology of the Land of the Bible.* New York: Doubleday, 1990.

McDowell, Josh. *The New Evidence That Demands a Verdict.* Nashville: Thomas Nelson Publishers, 1999.

McElroy, William D., and Carl P. Swanson, eds. *The Natural History of Man.* Englewood Cliffs, New Jersey: Prentice-Hall, Inc., 1973.

Muncaster, Ralph O. *Examine the Evidence: Exploring the Case for Christianity.* Eugene, Oregon: Harvest House Publishes, 2004.

Needleman, Jacob, A. K. Bierman, and, James A. Gould. *Religion for a New Generation.* New York: The Macmillan Company, 1973.

Olson, Everett C., and Jane Ann Robinson. *Concepts of Evolution.* Columbus, Ohio: Charles E. Merrill Publishing Company, 1975.

Pelikan, Jaroslav. *Whose Bible is It? A History of the Scriptures Through the Ages.* New York: Viking, 2005.

Penfield, Wilder. *The Mystery of the Mind: A Critical Study of Consciousness and the Human Brain.* Princeton, New Jersey: Princeton University Press, 1975.

Penrose, Roger. *The Emperor's New Mind: Concerning Computers, Minds and the Laws of Physics.* Oxford: Oxford University Press, 1999.

Peterson, Merrill D., ed. *James Madison: A Biography in His Own Words.* New York: Newsweek, 1974.

Pilbeam, David. *The Ascent of Man.* New York: The Macmillan Company, 1972.

Pritchard, James. B., ed. *The Harper Concise Atlas of the Bible.* New York: HarperCollins Publishers, 1991.

Reid, George J. *Canon of the New Testament.* The Catholic Encyclopedia, Vol. III, Online Edition, Accessed February 27, 2006, K. Knight, 2003.

Rue, Loyal. *Everybody's Story: Wising Up to the Epic of Evolution.* New York: State University of New York Press, 2000.

Sabom, Michael B. *Recollections of Death: A Medical Investigation.* New York: Harper & Row, 1982.

Sabom, Michael B. *Light and Death.* Grand Rapids, Michigan: Zondervan, 1998.

Schaefer, Henry F. *Science and Christianity: Conflict or Coherence?* Watkinsville, Georgia: University of Georgia Printing, 2003.

Schroeder, Gerald L. *The Science of God: The Convergence of Scientific and Biblical Wisdom.* New York: Broadway Books, 1997.

Schweitzer, Albert. *The Quest of the Historical Jesus.* New York: The Macmillan Company. 1960.

Smoot, George, and Keay Davidson. *Wrinkles in Time.* New York: William Morrow, 1993.

Strobel, Lee. *The Case for a Creator.* Grand Rapids, Michigan: Zondervan, 2004.

Stockman, Steve. *Walk On: The Spiritual Journey of U2.* Orlando, Florida: Relevant Books, 2005.

Tabor, James D. *The Jewish Roman World of Jesus.* University of North Carolina Charlotte (www.religiousstudies.uncc.edu), 2004.

Tacitus, Cornelius. *The Annals.* Translated by Alfred John Church and William Jackson Brodibb, The Internet Classics Archive (www.mit.edu).

Vermes, Geza. *The Complete Dead Sea Scrolls in English.* New York: Penguin Books, 1998.

Warren, Rick. *The Purpose Driven Life.* Grand Rapids, Michigan: Zondervan, 2002.

Watson, James D. *DNA: The Secret of Life.* New York: Alfred A. Knopf, 2004.

Weinberg, Steven. *The First Three Minutes: A Modern View of the Origin of the Universe.* New York: Basic Books, 1993.

Notes

[1] Cadet Prayer, The Citadel.
[2] The Cynical Web Site. "Religion." http://www.cynical.ws/definition/religion.
[3] The Skeptics' Guide to the Universe Transcripts. "Skeptical Quote Collection." Last modified February 15, 2014. http://www.sgutranscripts.org/wiki/Skeptical_Quote_Collection.
[4] The title of a book by Robert C. Fuller.
[5] Bayan, *The Cynic's Dictionary*, book cover.
[6] Fuller, *Spiritual but not Religious*, 2–5.
[7] PLoS One 8.8. "Beyond Reasonable Doubt: Evolution from DNA Sequences." August 2013. http://search.proquest.com/pringviewfile?accountid=322. Accessed Sept. 27, 2013.
[8] Bierce, *The Enlarged Devil's Dictionary*, 38.
[9] Charles Barsotti, *The New Yorker Collection*, The Cartoon Bank.
[10] The Skeptics' Guide, "Skeptical Quote Collection."
[11] Poets.org. "Sailing to Byzantium by W. B. Yeats." http://www.poets.org/viewmedia.php/prmMID/20310. Accessed Jan. 15, 2014.
[12] Fitzgerald, *The Rubaiyat of Omar Khayyam*, LXVI.
[13] Bartleby.com. "Invictus." http://www.bartleby.com/103/7.html. Accessed Jan. 20, 2013.
[14] Dana Fradon, *The New Yorker Collection*, The Cartoon Bank.
[15] BrainyQuote, "War Quotes - Page 2." http://www.brainyquote.com/quotes/topics/topic_war2.html. Accessed Dec. 15, 2013.

[16] "Skeptical Quote Collection." The Skeptic's Guide to the Universe Transcripts, www.sgutranscripts.org/wiki/Skeptical_Quote_Collection. Accessed Jan. 15, 2014.

[17] Mark 10:43–45.

[18] Jason Patterson, *The New Yorker Collection*, The Cartoon Bank.

[19] The siege of Dien Bien Phu resulted in the final defeat of the French army in 1954.

[20] Brainy Quote, Socrates, www.brainyquote.com/quotes/s/socrates163765.html. Accessed Jan. 5, 2014.

[21] Eric Teitelbaum, *The New Yorker Collection*, The Cartoon Bank.

[22] Goodreads. Bertrand Russell, http://www.goodreads.com/quotes/9473. Accessed Jan. 15, 2014.

[23] Bayan, *The Cynic's Dictionary*, 109.

[24] Maslow, *Motivation and Personality*, 35–58.

[25] Maslow, 164.

[26] Bierce, *The Enlarged Devil's Dictionary*, 45.

[27] The Cynical Web Site. "Conversion." http://www.cynical.ws/definition/conversion. Accessed Jan. 1, 2014.

[28] An RV resort business in Myrtle Beach, South Carolina.

[29] IZQuotes, Philip Massinger (1583-1640), http://izquotes.com/quote/251223. Accessed April 25, 2014.

[30] Bayan, *The Cynic's Dictionary*, 160.

[31] The Cynic's Sanctuary. "The Cynic's Dictionary." http://richardbayan.typepad.com/the_cynics_sanctuary/the-cynics-dictionary.html. Accessed Jan. 1, 2014.

[32] Dave Gardner (1926–1983). "Brother Dave" was a singer and comedian. This quote is paraphrased from my recollection.

[33] Bierce, *The Enlarged Devil's Dictionary*, 61.

[34] The Quotations Page. "Quotation Details." http://www.quotationspage.com/quote/24949.html. Accessed April 20, 2014.

[35] Bureau of the Census, *Statistical Abstract*, 70.

NOTES

36 The Quotations Page. "Quotation Details." http://quotationspage.com/quote/998.html. Accessed April 1, 2014.
37 The Skeptics' Guide, "Skeptical Quote Collection."
38 Smoot, *Wrinkles in Time*, 41.
39 Hawking, *Black Holes*, 89.
40 Smoot, *Wrinkles in Time*, 74.
41 Jack Ziegler, *The New Yorker Collection*, The Cartoon Bank.
42 Weinberg, *The First Three Minutes*, 8.
43 Ibid.
44 Smoot, *Wrinkles in Time*, 289.
45 From the Nobel Prize Citation, as reported in the *New York Times*, October, 4, 2006.
46 Smoot, *Wrinkles in Time*, 291.
47 Schaefer, *Science and Christianity*, 49.
48 Smoot, *Wrinkles in Time*, 17.
49 Strobel, *The Case for a Creator*, 138.
50 Smoot, *Wrinkles in* Time, 293.
51 Paul Davies interviewed by Phillip Adams on the ABC series, *The Creative Cosmos: The Big Questions*, 1995, 2002, published on ABC Science Online at www.abc.net.
52 Feynman, *The Meaning of It All*, 23.
53 Hawking, *A Brief History of Time*, 127.
54 Penrose, *The Emperor's New Mind*, 126.
55 Schaefer, *Science and Christianity*, 26.
56 Bayan, *The Cynic's Dictionary*, 66.
57 Genesis 1:25.
58 Dawkins, *The Selfish Gene*, 1.
59 Dawkins, *The Blind Watchmaker*, 6.
60 Sam Gross, *The New Yorker Collection*, The Cartoon Bank.
61 Public Acts of the State of Tennessee, House Bill No. 185 (March 13, 1925).

[62] Hanover College History Department. "Transcripts from *Tennessee versus John Scopes*, 1925." http://history.hanover.edu/courses/excerpts/111scopes.html.

[63] Olson and Robinson, *Concepts of Evolution*, 252–253. The quotes in this paragraph are from a textbook written by UCLA professors for college students, intended as "a general introduction to biology in the context of evolution."

[64] Audesirk, *Biology,* p.236.

[65] Feynman, *The Meaning of It All*, 16–17.

[66] Olson and Robinson, *Concepts of Evolution*, 29–30.

[67] Ibid., p. 53–56.

[68] Ibid., 180–189.

[69] Ibid., 208.

[70] Bayan, *The Cynic's Dictionary*, 59.

[71] The Cynic's Sanctuary. "The Cynic's Dictionary."

[72] Darwin, *The Origin of Species*, 484.

[73] Schaefer, *Science and Christianity*, 89.

[74] Ibid.

[75] *Life Science Weekly,* "Study Data from the National Aeronautics and Space Administration Provide New Insights into Prebiotics," Sept. 10, 2013, http://search.proquest.com/printviewfile?accountid=322. Accessed Sept. 27, 2013.

[76] Martin Schmieder and Fred Jourdan, "Cosmic Hotspots for Life," *Australasian Science,* Oct. 2013, http://search.proquest.com/docview/14360331537?accountid=322. Accessed Sept. 27, 2013.

[77] Center for Science and Culture. Steven C.Meyer, "DNA and Other Designs." April 1, 2000. http://www.discovery.org/a/200. Accessed April 20, 2014.

[78] Muncaster, *Examine the Evidence*, 91.

[79] Peter C. Vey, *The New Yorker Collection*, The Cartoon Bank.

[80] NewsRX Health. "Enzymes and Coenzymes; New Findings from the UNC School of Medicine Challenge Assumptions About Origins of

Life." October 6, 2013. http://search.proquest.com/docview/14368 88530?accountid=322. Accessed Sept. 27, 2013.
[81] Bierce, *The Enlarged Devil's Dictionary*, 192.
[82] BrainyQuote. "H. L. Mencken." http://www.brainyquote.com/quotes/quotes/h/hlmencke137237.html. Accessed Jan. 21, 2014.
[83] Barnes-Svarney, *New York Public Library*, 91.
[84] The Ediacaran fauna consisted of about one thousand specimens found mostly in Australia.
[85] Cambridge University, *The Cambridge Encyclopedia*, 371.
[86] Darwin, *The Origin of Species* Vol. II, 282.
[87] Olson and Robinson, *Concepts of Evolution*, 75–80. I go back to my text from the 1970s here because the authors, even though firmly committed to evolution and the certainty that science will eventually fill in any blanks, are especially honest in separating fact from theory. Many scientific (and religious) texts do not display this level of integrity.
[88] Gould, "Evolution's Erratic Pace." For more than thirty years, Gould was on the faculty of Harvard as professor of zoology, geology, biology, and history of science. He considered himself primarily a paleontologist and evolutionary biologist.
[89] David B. Kitts, "Evolution," *Paleontology and Evolutionary Theory* Vol. 28 (September 1974): 467. Kitts was a professor of geology and history of science at the University of Oklahoma.
[90] Pilbeam, *The Ascent of Man*, 2.
[91] John Hawks, Keith Hunley, Sang-Hee Lee, and Milford Wolpoff, "Population Bottlenecks and Pleistocene Human Evolution," *Oxford Journal of Molecular Biology and Evolution* (September 15, 1999), Accessed Oct. 24, 2013, http://mbe.oxford.org/content/17/1/2.full.
[92] Ibid.
[93] Britannica, *The New Encyclopedia Britannica*, Vol. 18, "Human Evolution."

94 W. Amos and J. I. Hoffman, "Evidence That Two Main Bottleneck Events Shaped Modern Human Genetic Diversity," *Proceedings of the Royal Society: Biological Science* (October 7, 2009), Accessed Oct. 24, 2013, http://rspb.royalsocietypublishing.org/content/early/2009/10/05/rspb.2009.1473.full.

95 Bierce, *The Enlarged Devil's Dictionary*, 196.

96 From a bumper sticker on a California SUV, as reported by Craig Hamilton.

97 Fischler, *Intelligence*, 31–2.

98 The figures cited in this paragraph are from Penrose, *The Emperor's New Mind*, 511, and Fischler, *Intelligence*, 58–9.

99 The Independent. "The 86 Billion Nerve Cell Question: Will We Ever Understand the Human Brain?" August 31, 2013. http://search.proquest.com/printviewfile?accountid=322. Accessed Sept. 27, 2013.

100 Ibid.

101 Fischler, *Intelligence*, 9.

102 Capra, *The Hidden Connections*, 43–44.

103 Rue, *Everybody's Story*, 82–5.

104 Mike Twohy, *The New Yorker Collection*, The Cartoon Bank.

105 Roger Penrose is foremost a mathematical physicist and has published with Stephen Hawking.

106 Penrose, *The Emperor's New Mind*, 531.

107 Ibid., 531, 540.

108 Ibid., 578–9. Penrose assumes that the mystery of human consciousness will be found in the eventual synthesis of quantum and classical physics.

109 Penfield, *The Mystery of the Mind*, 83.

110 Sabom, *Recollections of Death*; Sabom, *Light and Death*.

111 Sabom, *Recollections of Death*, 20.

112 Genesis 1:27.

113 Ecclesiastes 3:11

NOTES

[114] BU Anthropology. "Faculty Profiles: Matt Cartmill." http://www.bu.edu/anthrop/people/faculty/m-cartmill/ Accessed Feb. 15, 2014.

[115] "Skeptical Quote Collection." The Skeptic's Guide to the Universe Transcripts, www.sgutranscripts.org/wiki/Skeptical_Quote_Collection. Accessed Jan. 15, 2014.

[116] Bruce Eric Kaplan, *The New Yorker Collection*, The Cartoon Bank.

[117] Collins, *The Language of God*, 200.

[118] Paul Davies interviewed by Phillip Adams on the ABC series, *The Creative Cosmos: The Big Questions*, 1995, 2002, published on ABC Science Online at www.abc.net.

[119] Feynman, *The Meaning of It All*, 32.

[120] Psalm 19:1.

[121] Bierce, *The Enlarged Devil's Dictionary*, 264.

[122] "Skeptical Quote Collection," The Skeptics Guide to the UniverseTranscripts, www.sgutranscripts.org/wiki/Skeptical_Quote_Collection. Accessed Jan. 15, 2014.

[123] "Skeptical Quote Collection," Skeptics Guide to the UniverseTranscripts, www.sgutranscripts.org/wiki/Skeptical_Quote_Collection. Accessed Jan. 15, 2014.

[124] Bierce, *The Enlarged Devil's Dictionary*, 202.

[125] An accurate quote from Revelation 7:1.

[126] Ephesians 6:5.

[127] Peter Steiner, *The New Yorker Collection*, The Cartoon Bank.

[128] McDowell, *The New Evidence*, 8.

[129] The Cynical Web Site, www.cynical.ws/definition/conversion. Accessed Jan. 1, 2014.

[130] BrainyQuote. H. L. Mencken , www.brainyquote.com/quotes/quotes/h/hlmencke161245.html. Accessed Jan. 5, 2014.

[131] Charles Barsotti, *The New Yorker Collection*, The Cartoon Bank.

[132] Keller, *The Bible as History*, 157–162; Pelikan, *Whose Bible Is It?* 30. Precise dating of these events has not been possible. In the Cairo Museum, there is a monument from a mortuary temple near

Thebes dated to 1229 BC that mentions specifically Canaan and the "people of Israel," the first independent and contemporaneous documentation of the existence of Israel.

[133] Keller, *The Bible as History*, 279–80; confirmed in official records of the Babylonian royal house, translated by D. J. Wiseman in 1955 at the British Museum.

[134] Keller, ibid., 305–5, dates established in biblical passages referring to specific years in the reign of the Persian rulers Cyrus, Darius, and Artaxerses.

[135] Job 38.

[136] Ecclesiastes 3:11.

[137] Proverbs 1:7.

[138] Proverbs 4:7.

[139] Proverbs 4:18.

[140] Proverbs 16:18.

[141] Ecclesiastes 8:8.

[142] Isaiah 42:1, 42:6, 49:6, 60:3.

[143] Isaiah 53.

[144] Zechariah 9,12.

[145] Jeremiah 31.

[146] Pelikan, *Whose Bible Is It?*, 13–14.

[147] Deuteronomy 27:2–3.

[148] 2 Samuel 8:16.

[149] 2 Kings 22:10–11.

[150] Vermes, *The Complete Dead Sea Scrolls*, 11.

[151] Keller, *The Bible as History*, 376–9; Vermes, ibid., 12–14.

[152] Keller, ibid., 312–13.

[153] Godfrey Rolles Driver, "The Formation of the Old Testament," in Eiselen, *The Abingdon Bible Commentary*, 91–98; Pelikan, *Whose Bible Is It?*, 45–47. "Almost universal acceptance" alludes to what I believe are minor differences between Old Testament scriptures accepted by Protestants, Catholics, and Jews.

NOTES

[154] Keller, *The Bible as History*, 66–67; Pritchard, *The Harper Concise Atlas*, 17; Mazar, *Archaeology of the Land*, 184, 225. "When they came to Haran, they settled there"(Genesis 11:31). "He…made his way to the town of Nahor"(Genesis 24:10).

[155] Pritchard, *The Harper Concise Atlas*, 17.

[156] Keller, *The Bible as History*, 163–4; Pritchard, *The Harper Concise Atlas*, 28; Mazar, *Archaeology of the Land* 234.

[157] Pritchard, *The Harper Concise Atlas*, 71.

[158] Bierce, *The Enlarged Devil's Dictionary*, 39.

[159] In the fourth century, church historian Eusebius made AD 33 popular as the year of Jesus's death. Other scholars estimate the date differently within a few years. A definite range is set by the dates when Pontius Pilate was procurator, i.e., between AD 27 and AD 37.

[160] *Gospel* is an old English word meaning "good news," translated from the Greek word *evangelion*. The word was used by the apostle Paul in 1 Corinthians 15:1.

[161] Matthew 22:34–40; Jesus cites Deuteronomy 6:5 and Leviticus 19:18.

[162] Matthew 7:12.

[163] Matthew 9:13.

[164] Matthew 5.

[165] Matthew 20:26.

[166] Matthew 18:3.

[167] Matthew 17, Mark 9, Luke 9.

[168] Matthew 28:18; also see Mark 14:61–62 and Luke 22:70.

[169] John 1.

[170] John 1:17.

[171] John 3:16

[172] John 18:36.

[173] Matthew 16:18. The subsequent basis of papal authority.

[174] Minnen, Peter V., *Dating the Oldest New Testament Manuscripts*, Duke University Special Collections Library, Papyrus Archives, www.scriptorium.lib.duke.edu, December 12, 1995.

[175] Pelikan, *Whose Bible Is It?*, 115; Durant, *Caesar and Christ*, 616.
[176] Reid, *The Catholic Encyclopedia*, Vol. III.
[177] Ibid.
[178] Tacitus, *The Annals*, chapter XV (AD 62–65).
[179] Josephus, *The Works of Flavius Josephus: Antiquities of the Jews*, book 18, chapter 3.
[180] Tabor, *Josephus on Jesus*. Dr. Tabor is the chair of the Department of Religious Studies, University of North Carolina Charlotte.
[181] Lee Lorenz, *The New Yorker Collection*, The Cartoon Bank.
[182] Durant, *Caesar and Christ*, 557.
[183] Ibid., 557.
[184] Schweitzer, *The Quest for the Historical Jesus*, 399.
[185] Bayan, *The Cynic's Dictionary*, 171.
[186] Bierce, *The Enlarged Devil's Dictionary*, 159.
[187] The Quotations Page. Steven Weinberg's quote in the *New York Times,* April 20, 1999, http://www.quotationspage.com/quote/26814.html. Accessed Feb. 20, 2014.
[188] Madden, *God Wills It!*, 12.
[189] Frank Cotham, *The New Yorker Collection*, The Cartoon Bank.
[190] Durant, *The Reformation*, 209.
[191] Ibid., 210.
[192] Ibid., 208.
[193] Peterson, *James Madison*, 94–5.
[194] Bierce, *The Enlarged Devil's Dictionary*, 33.
[195] The Cynical Web Site, www.cynical.ws/wordsearch.php?word=atheist. Accessed Dec. 18, 2006.
[196] Matthew 18:3.
[197] Psalm 19:1.
[198] Romans 1:19–20.
[199] Genesis 1:26.
[200] Acts 17: 27.
[201] 1 Kings 19:11–13.

NOTES

[202] Frank Cotham, *The New Yorker Collection*, The Cartoon Bank.
[203] Romans 8:38–39.
[204] Thanks to Father Mark Goodman for this insightful analogy.
[205] *The Book of Common Prayer*, Prayers of the People, Form V, 391.
[206] Romans 3:23.
[207] John 21:17.
[208] "Skeptical Quote Collection," Skeptics Guide to the UniverseTranscripts, www.sgutranscripts.org/wiki/Skeptical_Quote_Collection. Accessed Feb. 19, 2014.
[209] Carl Sagan, Skeptics Guide to the UniverseTranscripts, www.sgutranscripts.org/wiki/Skeptical_Quote_Collection. Accessed Feb. 10, 2014.
[210] Matthew 5:3
[211] Cursillo is a program of the Episcopal Church designed for Christian leadership training and renewal. The format comes from Spain via the Catholic Church and has been adopted by other denominations as "Walk to Emmaus." The term means "short course." The focus of the weekend is a series of talks and meditations given by priests and laypeople.
[212] Matthew 18:3.
[213] There is much more to the complete Cursillo/Walk to Emmaus experience than I have mentioned.
[214] "Skeptical Quote Collection," Skeptics Guide to the UniverseTranscripts, www.sgutranscripts.org/wiki/Skeptical_Quote_Collection. Accessed Jan. 21, 2014.
[215] Famous Quotes. http://www.quotescentral.com.
[216] The Cynical Web Site, www.cynical.ws/wordsearch.php?word=decide. Accessed Dec. 22, 2006.
[217] Stockman, *Walk On*, 133.
[218] Paraphrase of Dave Gardner quote from my recollection.
[219] Kennedy, *Evangelism Explosion*, 17–18.
[220] Philippians 4:7. Changing the plural "hearts and minds" to singular.

221 George Gibbs, Washington Redskins coach, www.joegibbsonline.com.
222 BrainyQuote. "Francis of Assisi." http://www.brainyquote.com/quotes/quotes/f/francisofa109569.html. Accessed Jan. 25, 2014.
223 1 John 4:8.
224 John Eldridge wrote *Wild at Heart* mainly for men. He and his wife wrote *Captivating* for women.
225 Col. Robert Bell, a longtime friend and a great Christian.
226 Matthew 19:24.
227 Ephesians 2:10.
228 Ephesians 2:8–9.
229 The Cynical Web Site. "Expert." http://www.cynical.ws/definition/expert. Accessed Jan. 1, 2014.
230 Goodreads, "Cicero," http://www.goodreads.com/author/show/13755.Cicero

About the Author

Larkin Spivey is a decorated veteran of the Vietnam War and a retired Marine Corps officer. He commanded infantry and reconnaissance units in combat and was trained in parachute, submarine, Ranger and Special Forces operations. He was with the blockade force during the Cuban Missile Crisis and served President Nixon in the White House. As a faculty member at The Citadel, he taught courses in US military history, a subject of lifelong personal and professional interest. A committed religious skeptic for most of his life, he became a Christian at age fifty-three and has since written numerous books for skeptical readers about God's providential hand in American military history and the power of faith in war. He is not a minister or member of the clergy. He now writes full time and resides in Myrtle Beach, South Carolina, with his wife, Lani, and their extended family. He has made numerous television and radio appearances nationwide and speaks frequently to church, veteran, and other groups with his patriotic and spiritual message.

For more information about the author, his other books, and speaking engagements, visit: **www.larkinspivey.com**

Made in the USA
Columbia, SC
10 October 2018